PROPHETIC LIFESTYLE AN

Prophetic Lifestyle and the Celtic Way

ANDY AND JANE FITZ-GIBBON

MONARCH

Unless otherwise stated, biblical quotations are
from the New Revised Standard Version, 1989.

British Library Cataloguing Data
A catalogue record for this book is available
from the British Library.

ISBN 1 85424 385 3

Designed and produced by Bookprint Creative Services
P.O. Box 827, BN21 3YJ, England for
MONARCH PUBLICATIONS
in association with
ANGUS HUDSON LTD
Concorde House, Grenville Place, Mill Hill
London NW7 3SA.
Printed in Great Britain.

ACKNOWLEDGEMENT

We would like to thank all those who read the manuscript at various stages and made helpful comments. Also Tony and Jane Collins at Monarch, for all their help and encouragement.

The book would not have been possible without those friends of ours who have chosen to walk a prophetic lifestyle with us. It has been exciting, challenging, fulfilling and not a little scary!

Thanks and blessings. Let's go deeper . . .

CONTENTS

Preface	Making Connections	11
Chapter 1	When the Snow Melts	19
Chapter 2	Dance of the Eagle	27
Chapter 3	The Communicative God	43
Chapter 4	Snippets from History	57
Chapter 5	Dreams and Visions	71
Chapter 6	Parable and Prophetic Story-telling	85
Chapter 7	Prophetic Signs in John's Gospel	101
Chapter 8	Earthquake, Wind and Fire	113
Chapter 9	Swimming against the Flow	125
Chapter 10	Prophetic Intercession	135
Chapter 11	You Can All Live Prophetically	143
Chapter 12	Testing Prophetic Lifestyle	159
Chapter 13	Living with the Loose Ends	169
Notes		181
For Further Reading		185

MAKING CONNECTIONS

In the Christian church we are slowly beginning to awaken to
the fact that we live in what scholars have termed 'postmodernism'. The seeming certainties of the modern world
are proving to be fictional. A rational, scientific answer to all
problems, the inexorable movement of progress, the supre-
macy of Western culture over all others are being replaced
by a sense of uncertainty and meaninglessness. Philosophers
predict a 'new dark ages' of moral anarchy as Western
civilisation gives way to who knows what. Some even speak
of postmodern life as the end of history—there is nothing
more to come.

In the church, for some time, we have realised the barrenness of our spiritual life. We have not provided the answer to
the inner quest. Spiritually thirsty people have turned to the
New Age movement with its attempt to look beneath the
surface of life. Others have adopted philosophies and religions
which, on the face of things, present a deeper sense of
spirituality than found in the average Christian congregation.

At the same time, in the goodness of God, there have been stirrings towards a deeper and more satisfying spirituality. The charismatic movement has certainly helped. The great outpouring of the Holy Spirit associated with Toronto Airport Christian Fellowship has been far-reaching. There are rumours of revival in many nations.

Alongside the new things has been a search for rootedness in previous times of spiritual awakening. Guy Chevreau performed a good service for the current renewal movement in noting and documenting the similarities of the present move of God with that of the eighteenth-century awakening in New England.[1] In his second book he brought similar insights from the lives and teaching of Teresa of Avila and John Calvin.[2] To find roots is important to us. To know that others have 'passed this way before us' gives at least some sense of connectedness.

Celtic Christian communities

Yet 'a new dark ages' presents us with a greater challenge than faced by the church since the collapse of the Roman Empire. We can no longer assume even a passing awareness of Christian tradition and culture. The church's evangelistic task is towards a new paganism. In some senses the church has been here before. Spiritual darkness prevailed in Britain by the end of the fourth century. God began to bring light through communities of men and women who lived a radical, deeply spiritual, powerful and prophetic Christian life. It is no wonder that, in recent years, there has been something of a resurgence of interest in these early Christian communities. Many have found a resonance in seeking to follow Jesus in postmodernity with the stories of Celtic saints. Postmodern Christians have found a kindred spirit with Aidan and Columba, Hild and Bridet[3] (for the biblical feminists!) and of course Patrick.[4]

Interestingly, New Age devotees and Christians alike have looked back to see if the ancient mysteries of the Celts have anything to say to our generation. Of course, the two groups look back to different parts of the Celtic tradition. Some have found in the ancient Druid religion an earthy alternative to the high-pressured life of the 1990s. Some feminists have discovered a community life which was not always dominated by the patriarchy of the late middle ages and beyond. Here is a tradition that fills in the blanks and puts people in touch with the creation as nearly no other tradition has. The Celtic tradition resonates with the concerns of environmentalists, feminists, modern-day pagans and others who have found the collapsing late twentieth century liberalism, consumerism and individualism inadequate. The Celtic tradition tells a different story and many are making it their own.

We were first introduced to the Celtic tradition in 1989 in retreat on 'the Holy Island of Lindisfarne' with friends who were just beginning to explore spiritual roots in the 'ancient kingdom of Northumbria'. Holy Island is a small windswept island off the Northumbrian coast separated twice daily from the mainland as the cold waters of the North Sea cover the causeway. It was the first place in England where Christianity found good soil. In its barrenness there is a deep sense of the presence of God.

Celtic Christian communities flourished between the fifth and twelfth centuries, roughly from the time of Patrick's mission to Ireland (c461) to the conquest of Britain and Ireland by the Normans (1066 and 1169). Christianity had touched the British Isles through the Romans but had not really taken a deep hold on the populace. Those who were Christians tended to be of Roman stock and the indigenous Celtic peoples remained untouched by the new faith. When the Roman legions left, so largely did the Christian faith. However, in the Celtic reaches of the Empire a Christian faith with a slightly different heritage had begun to take hold, more akin to the Christianity of the East and the Desert Fathers and Mothers.

The Celtic Christian tradition is sometimes described as the Celtic Church in distinction from the Roman Church. However, we prefer to speak of 'communities' because the early British and Irish churches were far less organised than those which came later. It was never a unified organisational whole, but more of a network of Christians who shared similar emphases and values. Also, it would be a mistake to think of the church of the early mediaeval period (either Celtic or Roman) in denominational terms. There was a far greater sense of the universality of the church than we have known since the Reformation. The basic doctrines of the Celts were the same as the Romans (Trinitarian, orthodox). Yet there were a number of distinctive features which related to the inculturation of the faith at the western margin of Europe. In other words, the culture, thought patterns and experience of the Celtic peoples of Britain and Ireland gave to Christianity a flavour all of its own. It is these distinctive emphases which fascinate us as we engage the culture of postmodernism:

- The Celtic strand of Christianity was less hierarchical than the Roman and tended to be organised around monastic communities rather than parishes with fixed clerical structures.
- The leaders of the communities tended to be abbots or abbesses who oversaw the monastic work. Priests tended to be more like travelling evangelists who moved between different communities. Leaders could be either men or women and married priests were the norm rather

than the exception. Some monastic communities housed both sexes.

- There was a greater emphasis on the goodness of creation, and God was understood to be not merely transcendent, but also immanent in his world—not just above it, but also very much included within it, permeating all that he had made.

- There was an emphasis on simplicity of life and in some cases a great asceticism. This was often coupled with an emphasis on pilgrimage, wandering for the sake of Christ. Celtic Christians who left their homes, and all that was familiar, were known as the *peregrini*. They made hazardous journeys *pro amore Christi*—for the love of Christ. Voluntary exile from loved-ones and homeland was common and was known as white martyrdom.

- The Celtic Christians were aware of intense spiritual warfare. Stories are replete with power encounters between the light of Christ and the darkness of paganism. They had a sense of the spiritual powers associated with certain places both for good and for evil—blessing and cursing was stock-in-trade for Celtic missionaries. Angels and demons feature prominently in Celtic narrative and Celtic Christians developed a particular way of praying. The *caim* was a prayer of 'encircling', seeking the protection of God against the powers of darkness. The *lorica*, or 'breastplate', was another protective prayer, its most famous example being the prayer we know as Patrick's Breastplate.

- The Celts were also a very prophetic people. They had a great sense of the presence of God with them, within them and around them at all times. Theirs was a dynamic faith lived in the presence of God. God communicated with his people on a daily and very 'ordinary' basis.

There was no division perceived between sacred and secular. God was in all. Prophetic dreams and visions, healings and miracles were a large part of their Christian experience. They learned, perhaps more than any who followed them, what a creative imagination was.

It is this latter aspect of the tradition that we want to look at in this book, linking it with the current rediscovery of prophetic gifts in the church. In the beginnings of our reading of the Celtic saints we were impressed with their keenly developed sense of the way God communicated using the ordinary circumstances of life. It spoke to us of the way we had perceived God speaking to us in spiritual renewal and we began to feel connected with the early Celtic communities. We are glad to have rediscovered, with many in different traditions, the great store of wealth which has been hidden for so long.

However, we are aware of the danger of romanticising the past. Not everything we have read about Celtic Britain is good! The Celtic clans were warlike tribes who had a fierce rivalry with others to protect land and influence. Even the Christian Celts were prone to the political wrangling and infighting between rival tribes. There was a raw barbarism to much of their lives. We would be mistaken to try to recreate the Celtic past. Also, there is the danger of reading back our own assumptions into a previous era. It is very easy to pick out that which we like and ignore that which offends or challenges. That temptation has always been there, and the task of historical theology has often resembled a crude apologetic to buttress a denominational position. We need to be aware of the pitfalls.

In some ways we all choose the stories we wish to tell about ourselves. Stories define our self-understanding and give shape to our lives. A great part of the meaninglessness of postmodern culture is that there are no longer any convincing stories to live by. As Christians we are convinced of the central story of Jesus. Hollywood's cliché *The Greatest Story Ever Told* is actually profoundly true. That Western culture can no longer remember how to tell the story of Jesus is its greatest poverty.

For us, in the 'storylessness' of postmodern society, there is great benefit in seeing how the principal story of Jesus has affected others and how the story came alive for them. In the current renaissance of all things Celtic, we are discovering how a primitive people wove the story of Jesus into their own. In our narrative we are glad to include a resonance with the stories and tales of our Celtic forebears in the faith. We will be pleased if our lives are even a pale reflection of theirs.

Celtic saints mentioned in this book[5]

This list will help to put the names we mention throughout the book into some kind of historical space.

Boisil: mentor and soul friend to Cuthbert. He was a great prophet in the Celtic church.

Brendan the Navigator: 486–578. The saint who travelled, probably as far as the coast of North America.

Brigit: c452–c524. Most famous female leader in the Celtic communities. She was a spiritual guide to many.

Ciaran: 512–545. One of the 'Twelve Apostles of Ireland'. He founded the monastery of Clonmacnoise on the banks of the Shannon River.

Cuthbert: c634–687. Leader of the community at Lindisfarne. He spent many years in solitude on Cuthbert's Island and later on the Inner Farne. He was deeply loved by all those he served.

David (Dewi Sant): c520–c589. A soul friend and mentor of many saints.

Enda: The Abbot of Ardmere and friend of Brendan. Brendan received his blessing on his journey.

Ita: Sixth-century abbess. The most famous of Irish women soul friends after Brigit. She founded a monastery in County Limerick at Killeedy.

Kevin: d.618. Abbot of Glendalough, south of Dublin.

Funecha: Foundress of the monastery Clonbroney.

Patrick: c415–493 Born in either Scotland, England or Wales. Travelled to Ireland first as a slave and then as a missionary in c461. Christianity spread rapidly under his ministry in Ireland.

Samthann (Safan): d.739. First Abbess at the monastery at Clonbroney in Ireland and was a soul friend to many.

Sanctus (David's father): Welsh king and husband to **Non**, one of the greatest female saints.

CHAPTER I

WHEN THE SNOW MELTS

> Then all at once he did remember. It was the noise of running water. All around them, though out of sight, there were streams chattering, murmuring, bubbling, splashing and even (in the distance) roaring. And his heart gave a great leap (though he hardly knew why) when he realised that the frost was over.[6]

Like Edmund in C.S. Lewis's *The Lion, the Witch and the Wardrobe*, Christians around the world in the 1990s are beginning to suspect that the winter is over. Incredulous, and almost unwilling to believe the signs, it seems that there is a new outpouring of the Holy Spirit. Many believe it is perhaps the greatest visitation of God since the turn of the century which saw the Welsh, Azusa Street and Sunderland awakenings. Some believe it may be the beginning of a last great outpouring of the Spirit before Christ returns to earth. Preparations are being made for a great ingathering of new sons and daughters of the Father. There is a greater expectation in the air than most can remember—you can almost touch it. We hear the beginning of the sounds of springtime. . . .

St Patrick's 'power encounters' with the pagan druids are well known. In the great contest at Tara, centre of paganism in fifth-century Ireland, the druid Lucetmail challenged Patrick in much the same way that the prophets of Baal had challenged Elijah. Of the many feats performed by the druid, perhaps the most interesting came when Lucetmail brought snow all over the land to the depth of the waists of the onlookers. Patrick had already declined to perform the act, believing that the bringing of snow was contrary to God's will. Yet the power of darkness is limited and Lucetmail, though worker of the spell, could not remove the snow until the same time the next day. Patrick, realising that the druid could only perform evil and not good, responded by blessing the whole plain in the name of the Trinity. It is said that the snow disappeared without rain, mist or wind. A glorious sound of celebration was heard as the gathered crowd praised God in great amazement. The hearts of the people were touched. It was the beginning of a tremendous move of God in Ireland.

Winter wonderland

Our first winter across the Atlantic was not kind to the eastern seaboard of the United States. The blizzard of that year hit the eastern states with all the force of a volcano. The capital was shut down, no one could work. The state of Pennsylvania was declared 'closed'. Nothing opened and a $100 fine was imposed on any person foolish enough to attempt to drive a motor vehicle. New England noted the highest level of snowfall since records began. Temperatures dropped to $-18°C$ ($0°F$) with a wind chill taking it in places to $-32°C$ ($-25°F$). In those conditions human skin freezes in less than five minutes.

Up-state New York was spared the worst of the blizzards,

but still by mid-January sixty-seven inches of snow had fallen. Of course, our introduction to an American winter was not all bleak! We had our first ever truly white Christmas—it was wonderful. Huge flakes of snow were falling as we looked out of the window and opened our presents on Christmas morning. God had been exceedingly good to us.

But not too far away in our subconscious were a number of anxieties. We had been taken on a roller-coaster of a ride in which God had begun to open our eyes to spiritual realities we had only read about. His presence was near: we felt him often and he was teaching us to walk very close to himself. Ten months of incredible blessing gave way to a new period in our walk with God. God's abundant provision continued but became mingled with the most severe period of spiritual warfare we had ever experienced.

On that Christmas morning one of our latent worries was our son James' visa. We had arrived in the USA, in obedience to a prophetic call of God the previous September, using our business visas which we had obtained some years before. James was about to attend college and would some time within a few months need to change his visa status. We followed the advice we had been given by his new 'school', but things did not go smoothly. His visa petition was returned twice on purely administrative grounds, neither of which was a problem. The time factor was.

We had been greatly changed as a family by what had been termed the 'Toronto Blessing' and 20th January marks the anniversary of that great outpouring of the Holy Spirit. We had determined many months before to be in Toronto for the celebrations. We believed God wanted us to be there and we had made arrangements to see a number of old friends and some new ones we had made through the Internet.

The middle of January came with remarkable swiftness. Still no visa, and James could not cross the Canadian border without one. We marshalled a number of intercessors who we knew prayed for our ministry. We contacted local pastors and asked them and their folk to pray. Jane posted a message on the Net and we received encouragement from people all around the world. People we had never met sent messages telling us they were praying. Still no visa. We tried to exercise faith, but with an increasing worry which gnawed away at our spirits. Jane had determined that if the visa did not arrive she would remain in Ithaca with two of our children and Andy with our middle son, Ben, would travel with the fifty plus folk in our party. Even so, the celebration would be marred as the family would be divided.

We needed to leave on Thursday. On Tuesday Andy called the Immigration Service in Vermont. A kind and friendly assistant said that she wished she could help, and that the visa petition had arrived on an Inspector's desk. It sounded hopeful until she informed us that the process normally took fourteen days to complete from that particular point. Our spirits sank. We had only two days, but we continued to pray. Words were given by folk in our home church that the visa would come. Our closest friends told us not to worry, God was big enough. Hadn't we taught them not to doubt! We were being tested according to the things we had confidently proclaimed.

To our English sensibilities real cold was a new experience. As we were experiencing biting winds of $-25°F$ ($-18°C$) that cut through whatever clothing we wore, our 'Weekly Telegraph' (for all those Brits who need to keep up with the cryptic crossword, the football results and the goings on in parliament) told us that the UK was in the grip of

Arctic conditions. Temperatures had dropped to *plus* 25°F (−6°C)! Home-sickness did not help the waiting process.

As we waited for the visa petition the cold was unrelenting. Then, to everyone's surprise, on the same day Andy called the Immigration Service the weather changed. In one day the temperature rose through sixty-five degrees! The snow began to melt with incredible speed. We stood outside and simply listened. It sounded like a tropical rain forest. From roofs, trees, cars and down drains came a torrent of water. It felt as though spring had arrived three months too early. The fresh air, which the day before had stung the throat, now had the warm sweetness of a sunny April morning.

The thaw continued through Thursday morning. We sat together in the smaller of our two lounges with large windows to two sides, watching the astonishing thaw.

'I can't settle,' Jane commented, as we looked at one another across the room, hoping to see some sign of encouragement in each other's faces.

At quarter to ten a van pulled into the driveway of the house next door. There was no insignia on the sign of the vehicle to give any indication as to its purpose. The driver alighted and crossed the lawn thick with melting snow.

'Are you the Fitz-Gibbons?' he commented in the New York accent we had come to know well. 'Federal Express parcel for you.'

James' visa had arrived. The Immigration service had done in two days that which we were told would take two weeks. The snow continued to melt and we made our way to Toronto for, what was for us, a great weekend of worship and seeking God's will. Of the many times we have been to Toronto, this was perhaps the sweetest.

A new prophetic awareness

Our incident with the melting snow, the visa process and our awareness of the goodness of God demonstrates what we have learned to call 'prophetic lifestyle'. We are learning to find the voice of God in the ordinary (and not so ordinary) circumstances of life. We have become aware that our heavenly Father has a greater desire to communicate with us than we are, often, willing to listen to his voice. The boundaries between sacred and secular, natural and supernatural have become blurred as we have tried to walk closely with God.

The current worldwide spiritual awakening has produced a remarkable increase in the gift of prophecy in the people of God. As we prepared to move to the city of Ithaca NY, a prophetic minister had seen a picture in which snow covered the whole of Canada to a great depth. In the picture the snow covered even the highest mountains until there was a smooth plateau on the top. The picture changed as the warmth of the sun caused the snow to melt. A great torrent of water flowed from Canada into the northern states of the USA around the great lakes. The interpretation was that a spiritual awakening beginning in Canada would move southwards. It greatly encouraged us: if there was to be a great outpouring of the Spirit in the USA, perhaps we were to be part of it.

We had confirmation about the melting snow prophecy from a number of different sources. In mid-winter, in a renewal meeting—having battled through a blizzard to be there—a prophetic word was given that 'when the snow melts great blessings will come'. Over the winter weeks similar words were given a number of times by different people. One said that when the snow melted there would be a release of the power of the Spirit. Another that in a dynamic vision a great sound of cracking ice could be heard. Remarkably, there was confirmation through the Internet as a prophecy in New Hampshire was given virtually word for word the same as one we had heard in Ithaca. In January, just a week before we were to leave for Toronto, this was posted on the Internet:

When [the snow] melts:
Streams will become rivers
Rivers will become torrents of water
There will be flooding
Cellars will get water in them—touching us at home
Some houses will be swept away—without firm foundation
Some people will complain about the destruction
Some people will rejoice for spring and summer is near
Abundant supply of water. . . .

As we drove to Canada we marvelled at the way God had intertwined spiritual insight and the circumstances of life to communicate his great love to us. Some of our friends battled through floods to reach Toronto safely. Others left flooded basements in the knowledge that there was little they could do for a few days anyway. Some even rejoiced that their damp basements were worth the blessing that the thaw symbolised! God had allowed a break of forty-eight hours in one of the severest winters in recent years and spoke clearly to us through it. The local weather TV station termed it a 'freak window in the weather' as seventy-two hours later the deep freeze and snow returned. It was for us another lived demonstration of what we have come to call 'prophetic lifestyle'. Following Jesus had become an exciting, vibrant, nail-biting, edge-of-the-seat adventure which, for us, has mirrored stories in the Bible in its spiritual impact.

Esther de Waal comments on the Celtic saints that 'Here are

lives in which miracle is commonplace and in which the world of present reality is absorbed into an all-encompassing, all-pervading supernatural world.'[7] Could it be that in the late twentieth-century culture of postmodernism we might experience that same kind of dynamic Christian life? We believe so and will try to demonstrate why.

CHAPTER 2

DANCE OF THE EAGLE

A hedge of trees surrounds me, a blackbird's lay sings to me, praise I shall not conceal,
Above my lined book the trilling of the birds sings to me.
A clear-voiced cuckoo sings to me in a grey cloak from the tops of bushes,
May the Lord save me from Judgement; well do I write under the greenwood.[8]

One year during the spring and summer we became aware of God speaking to us in a variety of new ways. God was bringing us slowly and gently to a fresh way of perceiving his revelation. We had begun to think of it as 'prophetic lifestyle'. God would communicate with us in the ordinary, and sometimes bizarre, circumstances of our daily lives. To be sure, such impressions of God would be confirmed by Scripture and by sharing them with mature believers, but the immediacy of his speaking through natural things was new to us.

Birds as messengers from God

We have been fascinated by birds for a long time. We loved our times exploring the Northumberland coast during school holidays when the children were growing up and were thrilled when we saw a new species for the first time. We were, though, very amateur in our birding and couldn't by any means call ourselves 'twitchers' (but then who would!). We can't remember exactly how or when, but the birds became our friends and we would perceive God speaking to us in their appearance, their absence, and their behaviour.

The potency of symbol is often present in popular folklore. According to legend, when the last raven leaves the Tower of London, then England will fall. Of course, it's only a legend, but no one seems willing to take a chance and so ravens are brought to the Tower, their wings clipped, and a watchful eye kept over them by the Yeomen of the Guard, the Beefeaters. Merely a legend . . . but the ravens at the Tower have become a potent symbol of English national sovereignty.

Somewhere buried in our memory was something to do with birds not being around places of spiritual darkness. The children's books written by Alan Garner and published in the 1960s are set in Alderly Edge. They are full of magic and sorcery, and much is made of the fact that birds were infrequent visitors on the Edge—it was a place of deep secrets and dark things.[9] For some reason the birds stayed away from that which had the feeling and sense of evil about it. Also, we were aware that it is said that what strikes visitors to Auschwitz, where so many Jewish people were murdered, is the silence. There is no sound of birdsong. It is as if the birds, knowing the terrible things which took place, have since those days stayed

well away from the scene of gross inhumanity. Even the plant-
ing of fruit trees to attract them has had no effect.

It was a similar eerie silence that we noticed around our
new home on the outskirts of Ithaca NY. Set in, what looks like
from the air, a huge forest surrounding a beautiful lake, bird-
life flourishes. The world-famous Cornell University Labora-
tory of Ornithology is a mere half mile from where we live—
yet we became aware that we heard and saw no birds in the
many trees surrounding our new residence.

St Francis, friend of animals

Though new to us, 'prophetic lifestyle', where the ordinary
things of life become a means of God's communication, is not a
new thing. Many will recall that St Francis was known as a
friend of animals. Closeness to and regard for natural things
became a part of the developed Franciscan tradition. Some of
the stories of Francis are very tender. It is said that he became
attached to a little lamb given as a present to him because it
reminded him often of the Lamb of God. The lamb became for
Francis a prophetic sign pointing him beyond the natural order
to the invisible and eternal. Also, Francis rescued a pair of
doves which were to be sold and killed. His reason? That the
doves were innocent creatures likened in Scripture to pure
souls, full of faith and humility.

On one occasion, Francis stopped at the roadside to preach
to the birds. He noted their freedom and provision, urged them
to praise God, exulted in their songs as a gift from God and
exhorted them to love God all the more.

Thereupon the birds began to open their beaks and spread their
wings, they stretched out their necks and bowed their heads, and

with all kinds of noises and gestures showed how delighted they were with what he had said. Francis was so happy, praised God and invited them all to join in the praise. Then he made a great sign of the Cross over them all and sent them away; they all flew up into the sky with a great song, and Francis blessed them again with the sign of the Cross. They then divided into four groups, flying away to the four points of the compass. This was a sign that the brethren should preach the Cross to the four quarters of the earth, and, like the birds, should possess nothing, but trust entirely to God's providence.[10]

The things of nature, the songs and flight and behaviour of the birds became to Francis a prophetic sign. God communicated with him through the birds.

There are many instances of Francis's affinity with the birds, where God used them as the instruments of his speaking. One such instance concerns a falcon, where the bird was used to show God's loving care and concern. Francis was spending some time in a hermitage, in total isolation, when he befriended the falcon. God used the falcon to become Francis's alarm clock!

For always during the night it announced with its song and noise the hour at which the saint was accustomed to rise for worship of God. This was very pleasing to the saint of God, in that, by reason of the great solicitude of the bird for him, any delay on his part because of laziness was driven away. But when the saint was afflicted more than usual by illness, the falcon would spare him and not give the signal for the time of the watches. Indeed, as if instructed by God, it would very gently sound the bell of its voice about dawn.

Two ravens from God

Such stories cannot and should not be relegated to the mists of history. If God could use the birds to communicate with Francis we might expect the same today.

God used ravens to demonstrate his love and concern for a friend of ours in a time of sickness. Kathleen, an Episcopalian priest, neighbour and good friend of ours shared an interesting story with us:

> In the spring I had intestinal bleeding, which the doctor said needed to be investigated, by a colonoscopy, to check for possible tumours or polyps. Two days before the colonoscopy, two large ravens—not crows, but ravens—were flying back and forth early in the morning between the church and the rectory. One even hovered momentarily with its wings spread right outside the front bedroom window as my son was waking up, so that he saw it also. It seemed to me that the ravens were an ambiguous sign. I was momentarily tempted to take their presence as a bad omen, when it came to me very strongly that in the Bible, ravens came to feed the prophet Elijah in the wilderness (1 Kings 17). About ten that morning, a friend who is a Pentecostal pastor called me on the telephone. He had not known that I was sick, but said that God had brought me to his mind in prayer. I told him about the medical problem and about the ravens; and he and his wife drove up fifty miles that evening to visit me in the rectory; then we went over to the church and they prayed with me for healing. The colonoscopy two days later showed no tumours or polyps but only some evidence of an acute infectious colitis which was already resolving, and has never recurred. Since Jesus in Matthew 15:26 calls healing and deliverance 'the children's bread', to me, the two ravens were a sign of my two friends bringing me prayer for healing in a time of need.

Kathleen's story is full of insight on the prophetic lifestyle.

- She was aware of circumstances and happenings around her. She noticed the ravens. So many things happen to all of us which we simply allow to pass by without a second thought. Awareness is important.
- She considered what she had observed and experienced in the light of the Scriptures.
- She received the ravens as a sign and communication of God's goodness to her.

Anoint with oil in the name of the Lord

We had been meeting with Christians from a number of churches to pray for God to bring renewal to the church. We had experienced renewal in the UK very powerfully and were longing for the same in the USA. But it had been a struggle. It seemed to us that the 'new wine' was not flowing and we wrestled with God as to the reasons. It was during this time that the birds became God's messengers to us. We had seen none in our garden and it worried us. It spoke to us of continuing darkness.

We determined to anoint our new home with oil in the name of Jesus. A close Anglican friend assured us of the benefits of this 'sacramental' activity. We had experienced it before with quite dramatic results and so we set about our task. We anointed each door and window, first on the ground floor; then inside each room downstairs, then the upper level and finally the basement. We prayed through the whole house. Then we turned to the garden. Our home is one of eight on a three-acre site, built only a couple of years ago in what was a small forest. The building company was sensitive to the natural environment and many trees still remain. We anointed the large stones which line the driveway, particularly those at the entrance to the drive. As we prayed, we asked the Lord to send the birds.

The next morning, as we prayed and looked over the trees in our garden, we were unprepared for the sight that met us. There was movement.

'Andy, look, I think we've got the first bird,' Jane commented.

White-breasted nuthatches are unmistakable in their eating habits. At first appearance they are somewhat similar to a great tit, except they walk upside down along the tree trunk, pecking away at the bark with their sharp little beaks.

'Thank you Lord! You answered us,' we continued to pray.

Then there was more movement, and then more, and still more. In the space of five minutes as we watched and prayed we saw two varieties of woodpeckers, chickadees, nuthatches, junkos, mourning doves and sparrows which all seemed to appear from nowhere.

'Lord, you have answered our prayers. Now show us what these little birds mean.'

A warning from God

We noticed a pattern. It didn't always fit, but the fit was remarkably accurate on too many occasions for us to simply cast it aside. The birds represented people. On the days of renewal meetings we would watch our bird garden to see how birds would appear. We began to notice that when there were many birds we would have a larger number of folk at the renewal meetings we were hosting. When there were fewer birds we noticed a correspondingly lower attendance at the meeting.

We also noticed the new birds. A new bird meant the appearance of someone new or some new group within the meetings. The cardinal is an unmistakably bright red bird about the size of an English thrush. Its brilliance catches the eye and it is very difficult to turn away from its startling beauty. One fine day in early autumn brought our first northern cardinal. We had joked about the cardinals being Catholic and Episcopal (Anglican) friends. That evening the new folk seeking God were from both Catholic and Episcopal churches. We were astonished!

'Look Mummy, there are the Cornell birds again,' Rebekah commented, pointing at the half dozen or so crows with red tabs on their wings.

'Why do you call them Cornell birds?' Jane responded.

'Because they belong to Cornell of course. Look they have Cornell tickets!' Rebekah replied, as if everyone already ought to know.

Sure enough, the crows are part of a study being carried out by graduate students at Cornell University. The birds are caught and tagged with different coloured patches to their wings so behaviour and movement can be studied. Our birds were tagged with red patches. That evening we had, for the first time, a good representation from one of the Christian groups on Campus.

'Cindy, we saw this beautiful large bright blue bird with a white breast and a dark crest on its head,' Jane enthused.

Cindy and Dave are our 'mentors' as far as birds are concerned. They have been keen bird-watchers for many years and know just about everything there is to know about birds in the north-east USA. By this time we wanted to know all we could about the birds who had become for us friends and messengers from God. We pressed Cindy for some tidbit of information which might help us.

'The bluejay is the watchmen for the other birds,' began Cindy. 'See what happens. Whenever there is an approaching stranger or some noise or disturbance it will always be the bluejay who sees it first and lets out its distinctive squawk. When the bluejay signals, the other birds heed the warning and you will see them fly off.'

We have watched that phenomenon many times. We have taken the bluejay as signifying for us some warning from God. When they appear it sends us to prayer. 'Lord, is there something we need to be careful about? Are you warning us of some impending trial?'

Brendan's voyage

Since we began to discover God's voice to us in our bird garden we have realised that others in previous periods of the church had made a similar discovery. Brendan, the Celtic saint famous for his journeying, lived between 486 and 578. Edward Sellner tells the story of Brendan. There is an instance on Brendan's famous voyage to the Island of Paradise.

At that moment they sat down to eat, a bird alighted on the prow of the ship and made music as sweet as an organ with its wings, beating them on the side of the boat. Then Brendan perceived that it was telling them something, and he listened as the bird spoke: 'On this journey four seasons have been determined for you; that is, the Day of the Lord's Supper is to be celebrated with the holy man, Easter on the island, which is really the back of a sea monster, and from Easter to Pentecost with a son on Paradise Island, and Christmas on the Island of Ailbe up to Mary's feast of Candlemas. At the end of the seventh year you will reach the land you are seeking, and you will be there forty days and then back to your homeland.' On hearing this Brendan lay on the ground, wept, and gave praise and thanks to God the Creator of all things. The bird returned to its own place, the holy man departed leaving his blessing with them. . . .[11]

Schooled in a liberal scientific education (for which we are, incidentally, most grateful!), it is somewhat hard for us to read stories like that of Brendan's voyage. We want to ask questions like 'Is it true?' 'Do birds really talk to people?' 'Surely, our experience would lead us to treat the story as a mere legend, something dreamed up out of a fertile medieval imagination?' In many ways they are the wrong questions to ask, just as to ask scientific questions of Genesis 1 is inappropriate. Though our world-view has enriched us in many ways, it has also made us poverty stricken in other ways. Whatever the 'historical truth' of Brendan's adventure, we have a story in which a saint of God is helped through some difficulty by finding God's revelation through a simple bird which alights on his ship. There is amazing power in the story which touches us at levels that scientific rationalism does not come near. Our twentieth-century Western questions like 'Can it be proved?' and 'Is it true?' need to be supplemented with other questions such as 'Where is God in this?' and 'Can we hear his voice here?' We are beginning to learn to look at life differently.

Kathleen, our Episcopal friend, shared with us another story about God using birds to direct her. She was booked to preach at a small remote church. Unfortunately, she had misplaced the directions the pastor had sent her, although she possessed a map of the area. Eventually she realised she was lost, and prayed, 'Lord, I'm lost, please send an angel or guide me somehow.'

As she spoke a flock of about twenty-five pigeons took off,

going down the road to the right. Our friend followed, eventually reaching another intersection, where the same thing happened. Again, the birds indicated direction by their flight patterns. This time as she followed she found herself led to the church she was looking for. Kathleen shared a wonderful testimony of God's guidance with the congregation that Sunday morning!

Prophetic dance of the eagle

Prayer walking is good for you. It exercises your heart, lungs and legs. It's good for the kingdom of God too. It exercises your spiritual capacity and *exorcises* the odd demon!

We love Taughannock Gorge. It is a steep ravine situated on the west side of Lake Cayuga some seven miles from the city of Ithaca. On each side of the gorge impenetrable rock rises like a solid wall some four hundred feet. Taughannock Falls, itself, though considerably narrower than Niagara, is actually higher at 215 feet. It is a place of unspoilt natural beauty. We have walked the gorge trail in each of the four seasons. In the summer it is a place of luscious vegetation, with warm water caressing your toes as you walk along its three-quarters of a mile length. In the autumn the trail is a golden blaze of reds and browns giving way to the deep snow of winter when the falls are frozen solid. The sheet of ice produced by the spray of the falls gives a visual display of a myriad of blues and greens which delights the senses. In springtime the force of the water as the snows melts is almost frightening. In the spring a sturdy wood and metal bridge was simply swept away under the power of the raging torrent.

Besides being a very beautiful place, Taughannock was also the site of two Native American villages and the place where a chief of the Delaware tribe was murdered. We had begun to walk the gorge trail praying that any spiritual strongholds associated with its history would be broken in Jesus' name. There is much work to be done in prayer around these sites of human inhumanity. We were particularly concerned with what may have been curses placed on the land by practitioners of animistic religion and by the thoughtless brutality of white people in taking land and devastating native villages.

The beauty of Taughannock was matched (for us at least) by a certain 'eeriness'. There was one particular spot on the trail that was always icy cold. Even when the general air temperature was in the eighties, the cold wind at this particular spot would send a chill through us. The gorge was another place where we had seen few birds and it worried us. We walked the gorge trail many times and prayed as we did that God would break spiritual strongholds and release the life of the Holy Spirit. We prayed that God would send the birds as a sign to us that the enemy's power was broken.

Many of our prayer walks seemed apparently fruitless. One day, however, as we walked we sensed something different. First, we noticed that the usual cold spot was uncannily warm. Then we noticed a little bird, then another, then another crossing our path as we made our way along the trail.

'Do you think this might be a sign that there is to be a spiritual breakthrough?' Jane commented with some excitement. 'Let's pray that the Lord confirms it.'

We walked on with expectancy, sensing the presence of God as we did so. For some reason, when we reached the end of the trail, we both looked up at the same moment. The walls of the gorge towered above us as we looked at the still blue sky. A small flock of birds flew in formation from one of the trees high on a cliff. Then we saw it.

As if out of nowhere, its huge wingspan lifted it on a current of air. Its white head and tail were unmistakable. Its beauty staggering. The majesty of its flight breathtaking. We were gazing on a bald eagle as it danced before us in the autumn sky. We sat transfixed for about ten minutes as the eagle danced and dived with consummate grace.

We had come to equate the eagle with the prophetic ministry and God's sign that day was clear to us. Spiritual strongholds in the Finger Lakes region were being broken. There was to be a great breakthrough. He had sent his eagle to confirm what we had begun to sense in the Spirit.

About the same time we tried to discover more about the Native Americans who had once lived in the Finger Lakes region. The Iroquois nation were a proud people with a rich culture long before white Europeans took their land. We wanted to try to understand. We wanted to read their stories and uncover what it was that had led the 'white man' to so mercilessly destroy these ancient people.

Our search took us to the local bookshop where we avidly scanned the shelves. Jane's eye was caught by a book with the title *Wisdomkeepers*. The book contains conversations with elders and spiritual leaders of First Americans all around the States. Many of the stories are moving and contain wisdom not far removed from and often very close to biblical revelation. Reading the book demonstrated to us again that Paul's words in Romans are true. God has left himself a witness in every people group of the world.

Sadly, the stories also radiate with the pain of people too often misunderstood and often abused. As we have read and reread these stories we have longed for a time when reconciliation will be made in Christ's name and when forgiveness is extended and received and when native peoples will look to

Jesus as Messiah, son of the Great Spirit. There is much work and much prayer needed as it was often in God's name that atrocities were perpetrated and wrongs done.

In that bookshop as Jane scanned the page she could hardly contain her amazement. One of the stories tells of a gathering of the Lakota people in 1983. They gathered at Wounded Knee, the place of a massacre in 1890 when 250 men women and children were cruelly executed. It was the place of further troubles in 1973, ending in more bloodshed. Frank Fools Crow, a ninety-three-year-old spiritual leader led the gathered company in prayer to the Great Spirit. The elder asked the creator for a sign that he still loved his Indian children. When the prayer was finished the most amazing thing happened.

> People nudge each other in awe. 'Look! Look up in the sky!' someone cries. Our eyes raise skyward with the others, and there, perhaps a thousand feet above our heads, circling, circling on outstretched wings, the only thing visible in all that colossal blue dome of sky—an eagle! . . . For fully ten minutes the great bird, witness of the Creator, hovers over the sacred hill of Wounded Knee. Then, before tears can be wiped from wondering eyes, it suddenly flies off and almost instantly disappears, gone whence it came. And the elder thanks the Creator for recognising the people once again by sending—as He has often done before—the Sign of His power and love.[12]

We have since walked the Taughannock trail many times. Like children who had passed into Narnia through a certain doorway, we have looked longingly heavenward to catch a sight again of our 'prophetic eagle'. We have never seen it since. It has almost an imaginary, dreamlike quality to it. People have asked us since, 'Are you sure it was an eagle?' We have scanned the books, looked at the pictures, pondered the flight pattern and we remain convinced. God revealed again his immense grace and his wonderful plan through a wonder of nature.

All this stuff and nonsense about birds! It may seem fanciful to some readers and we wouldn't want to give the impression that every bird we see has some prophetic significance. Nor will our experience be the same for others. Naturally, some people enjoy birds and some are indifferent. Some think of them as pests—look what mess a seagull can make of a newly washed car! But we are saying that for us the birds stand as an illustration of how God, in the whole of our lives, can reveal himself in ever more wonderful and diverse ways. As we have tried to hear God and find God in the whole of our lives, the habits, patterns, appearance and absence of birds has taken on a particular significance.

The Celtic tale of Kevin and the blackbird makes a fitting ending to a chapter on birds. It is said that, one Lent, Kevin was at prayer with his arms outstretched when a blackbird came to rest on his opened hand. The birds began to nest and laid her eggs in the warmth. Kevin, moved with concern for the bird, did not change his posture until the eggs were hatched. An angel appeared to him and urged him to move position. Kevin replied that if his saviour could hold out his hands upon a cross to bear the pain of the world, then Kevin could endure the discomfort he felt on behalf of the blackbird.[13]

CHAPTER 3

THE COMMUNICATIVE GOD

Prophetic ministry is the declaration of the mind of God in the power of the Spirit, with a special bearing on the current situation.[14]

Professor F.F. Bruce

Close to the heart of being a Christian, a follower of Jesus Christ, is to know and experience a personal relationship with God, to know God's presence. We have believed that for a long time: it is a staple element in the diet of the whole Christian world. Ever since John Wesley expressed his experience of God as the 'heart strangely warmed', evangelical Christians have desired to enter a similar experience. We have made the personal encounter with God in conversion the basis for all else in the Christian life. We understand that to be a Christian is more than just a knowledge of Christian teachings comprehended with the mind. It is more like knowing an intimate friend; it is the knowledge of relationship rather than book-learning.

This book is about that: making sense of knowing God,

which is the most important pursuit we could ever have. To know God has been our preoccupation for all of our adult lives. However, we do not admit to being very good at it. In fact, in the last few years we have been on an accelerated course in aspects of knowing God which has, at times, staggered us. We have discovered and rediscovered things which we should have known all along, but somehow missed, misplaced or ignored. Still, we feel we have ventured only a few tentative steps. We have no firm conclusions. One of the values we embrace within our network of home-based churches is that of provisionality. There are no 'ten easy steps to knowing God profoundly'. But we do feel we know him better. God is greater, more mysterious and awesome than we have understood before.

We are learning something about what we are calling 'prophetic lifestyle'. It is the discovering of God in our everyday lives. Prophetic lifestyle is to live in the 'now' of God's presence. It is to find a daily communication with God through the Spirit which includes all of our senses and all the circumstances of our lives. It is being unwilling to compartmentalise spiritual life and to reduce it to Sunday mornings and quiet times. It is being unwilling to live with the dualism of the sacred and the secular. We no longer want to make a division in our lives between holy and profane. Whether we are in prayer or at work, reading the Bible or at leisure, in a service of worship or making love—all is lived in the presence of the Father.

If to be spiritual is only to be in church or reading the Bible then the pressure is on to do more of those things. The rest of life becomes a second best, unworthy of God. The resultant tension can prove for some almost unbearable. For others it produces a kind of 'super-spirituality' which few can live up to.

Too many Christians live a kind of double life. Their lives are filled with pressure and guilt: they are somewhat confused. Prophetic lifestyle is to know that our heavenly Father is in every aspect of our lives and will use all we do, all that we are and all that happens to us to show us his love and goodness. In theological terms we might say that prophetic lifestyle is knowing the immanence of a transcendent God—the eternal, infinite and powerful realised in the temporality, finitude and weakness of ordinary, everyday life.

The idea of prophetic lifestyle has become very precious to us. It is finding that our Father delights to communicate with us and reveal himself in all manner of fresh ways. Indeed, it is only in so far as God discloses himself that we *can* know him. Is it that the revelation of God is greater today? We don't think so. But in God's goodness he has graciously opened our eyes to see more of him. Eugene Peterson translates one of the beatitudes in this way: 'You're blessed when you get your inside world—your mind and heart—put right. Then you can see God in the outside world.' (Matthew 5:8.)[15] In some small measure we have begun to discover 'God in the outside world'.

Revealed religion

In the best theology it has always been recognised that the whole of life is about grace. Undeserved and unmerited by any human being, the infinite and perfect God has chosen to reveal himself to his sinful creatures. God has always taken the initiative, and he always will. He loved us before we knew him; he loved us when we were still his enemies. Like Abram before his call we were all those who worshipped 'foreign' gods. When God stepped into our lives 'to reveal his Son in me', as Paul expressed it in Galatians 1:15, there was nothing about us to merit his love and favour. His self-disclosure to us arose out of his wonderful, endless and unfathomable love.

A moment's reflection on how any of us came to faith places this right in our experience. Many of us were taken by surprise when God came looking for us. He came through a friend or through something we read or through a life-circumstance. Even those of us who went seeking God had a desire to do so placed within us by God himself. Being a Christian is by nature a gift—there is a givenness about it. It was what the church fathers termed 'prevenient grace'. God is always at work around us and in us before ever we become aware of him or start to seek him.

Without doubt, there is a great mystery in all this. Infinite God—finite people. Holy God—sinful creatures. The gulf is indeed great. It is further complicated in that God is also invisible. How on earth are we to get to know, to understand and enter into a relationship with that which is invisible, unless the invisible makes itself known, a self-revelation? That self-disclosure of God is at the very heart of Christian faith.

But in what ways does God choose to reveal himself? We must, of course, start with the statement that God is revealed in the Scriptures. Christianity, as a revealed religion, is very much a 'religion of the book'. In sacred scripture are found the stories of how God interacts with people in real historical situations. In the Bible there is the Spirit-inspired sacred wisdom of a people (Israel) and the first witnesses to the Messiah (the apostles). If you want to find out about God—what he is like, his character, his ways, the things he desires in his people—you need only look to the pages of the Bible. The Bible is the 'sufficient' guide to teach us about God. Christians go so far as to say that the Bible is a complete revelation, meaning that there is nothing left to be revealed about God other than that which is already there.

But we do need to exercise care. We cannot say that to know the Bible is to know God, for many unbelievers know the content of the Bible with no personal knowledge of God. James tells us that the demons believe and tremble but do not have a true knowledge of the living God (James 2:19). Bible knowledge must be enlivened by the revelation of the Spirit of God.

Revealed beyond the Scriptures

However, in the two central streams of Western Christianity (the Catholic and the Reformed) place has always been given to revelation which is not directly from the Bible, based on passages such as Paul in Romans 1:19–25—

> For what can be known about God is plain to them, because God has shown it to them. Ever since the creation of the world his eternal power and divine nature, invisible though they are, have been understood and seen through the things he has made. So they are without excuse; for though they knew God, they did not honour him as God or give thanks to him, but they became futile in their thinking, and their senseless minds were darkened. Claiming to be wise, they became fools; and they exchanged the glory of the immortal God for images resembling a mortal human being or birds or four-footed animals or reptiles. Therefore God gave them up in the lusts of their hearts to impurity, to the degrading of their bodies among themselves, because they exchanged the truth about God for a lie and worshipped and served the creature rather than the Creator, who is blessed for ever!

In many ways the passage is somewhat negative, but it does help us see that there is an understanding in the Bible that

God reveals himself in ways other than through the Scriptures. Creation, the natural world around us, is in some respects a guide to knowing God.

In the Catholic, Thomistic tradition (after Thomas Aquinas), this kind of revelation was called 'natural law'. God revealed himself through nature in such a way that every person on the planet could know him, even those who had never read the Scriptures. To be sure, that knowledge was partial, basic and incomplete. But God could be known. In the Reformed tradition understanding centres around the ideas of 'general' and 'special' revelation. Special revelation is the way God has revealed himself in the Scriptures. General revelation is the way that God has revealed himself through the creation. In the beauty of creation, the intricacies of the human body and the expanse of the stars you will find a revelation of God.

In both traditions revelation through nature needs to be supplemented by the Scriptures for people to come to a deep and true knowledge of God. In this there is a good balance. People who discern there is a God by looking at created things may find themselves in error when it comes to a full knowledge of salvation. For example, the truth of death and resurrection is seen clearly in the cycles of nature. Jesus said as much when he alluded to a grain of wheat falling into the ground to die, only to bring forth much more fruit (John 12:24). However, the revelation given in nature is completed only through a consideration of the story of Jesus—his life, death and resurrection are not found outside of the Scriptures. Nature points to it but is incomplete without the full knowledge of God in Christ. Nevertheless, the revelation of God in nature is a part of God's self-disclosure which we need to be more in touch with again.

Eternity in their hearts

Is it possible that in every culture the whole world over God has given a witness of himself? Don Richardson believes so. His profound book *Eternity in Their Hearts*[16] (from Ecclesiastes 3:11) demonstrates how in many pre-Christian cultures there is evidence of divinely revealed truth which fits well with the revealed truth of the Bible. Indeed, Richardson suggests that pre-Christian truth was by way of preparation for the fullness of revelation in Jesus.

It's a sad testimony that much missionary zeal simply ignored native cultures, believing them rightly to be pre-Christian but ignoring the revelation of God within them. The missionary task is carried out better when Christians look for that which is of God already within a culture and then demonstrate that Jesus is the fulfilment of all the good which is already there. This is not, of course, saying that native cultures are free from idolatry and falsehood, but rather that in all cultures there is a revelation of God which we can affirm as well as error to challenge.

Two instances of this might help; one from the Old Testament and one from the New. Genesis 14 presents us with the mysterious entrance (and disappearance!) of Melchizedek on the biblical scene. He is clearly not, according to the Genesis genealogy, among the people of God in the line of what became known as Israel. Melchizedek was a righteous Canaanite priest who offered a blessing to Abram in the name of El Elyon, God Most High.

Blessed be Abram by God Most High,
maker of heaven and earth;
and blessed be God Most High,
who has delivered your enemies into your hand!

(Genesis 14:19–20)

But the revelation of God as El Elyon was not the revelation of God as Yahweh (God's covenant name to Israel). It was, nonetheless, a profound and true revelation of God. It was sufficiently recognised as *of God* that Abram pays the tithe to Melchizedek. Melchizedek represents those who don't have the special revelation and understanding of Jewish or Christian Scriptures but who, nonetheless, have some revelation of God. Abram received this revelation gratefully.

In Acts 17 Paul is faced with a new challenge. Before that time he had ministered mostly to Jewish people in the setting of the synagogue. He had begun to venture further afield and interested gentiles had listened and had begun to follow Jesus. In Athens he is faced, for the first time, with Greek culture at its peak before the learned and respected Areopagus. Paul, the master of con-textual evangelism, on this occasion does not begin with the Jewish Scriptures. That approach was fine for those with a work-ing knowledge of Jewish tradition. But in the centre of Greek learning, Paul begins his evangelism right where the philoso-phers are—with their own philosophy, 'so that they would search for God and perhaps grope for him and find him—though indeed he is not far from each one of us. For "In him we live and move and have our being"; as even some of your own poets have said, "For we too are his offspring"' (Acts 17:27–28).

The two quotes in verses 27–28 come from the Cretan poet Epimenides (c315–240 BC) and the Cilician poet Aratus (c331–233 BC). Paul uses this Greek wisdom favourably, recognising it as truth. Skilfully he presents an argument in which they would agree with him and points to the truth of God within their developed culture. He uses even their own poets and philosophers, and suggests that Jesus Christ is the fulfilment of all that they have learned.

Paul's approach is full of lessons in how to win those who

are not schooled within the Judeo-Christian tradition and might well stand for a model for us as we grapple with postmodern society. Of the many lessons we want to highlight just one: Paul was very clear that even these pagan Greek philosophers had within their tradition revelation from God. It was not all untruth. God could be found amid their reasoning and creativity. In other words, they had been given a measure of truth and all truth is God's truth.

The Celtic Christian communities in Britain and Ireland were very aware of the culture they ministered in. Many of the themes of their pre-Christian pagan lives carried over into their new faith without much difficulty. Ian Bradley quotes Taliesin, a sixth-century Welsh bard, as saying, 'Christ the Word was from the beginning our Teacher, and we never lost his teaching. Christianity was in Asia a new thing, but there was never a time when the Druids of Britain held not its doctrines.'[17]

We might draw either of two conclusions from this statement: that Christianity was so watered down in its Celtic version that it still resembled paganism, or that before the gospel was ever preached to the pagan Celts they had already been prepared by God for the message to come. We prefer to think the latter is true. In their culture and understanding there was much that was of God and which pointed, like a signpost, to the truth of God in Christ.

The easier path is to decry all pre-Christian and non-Christian culture as bad. To look for that which is of Christ, and therefore to be affirmed, needs careful discernment. There is a risk involved, but we believe, as the Celtic Christians did, that the risk is worth taking.

Truth in native cultures

'Jim, we believe God might be calling us to Ithaca, New York.'
We had arrived a little late to transport Jim Paul to the conference which was now in its second day.

'Don't say any more! I have seen this in a vision three weeks ago.'

When we had parked in the leisure centre car park Jim could contain himself no longer. He shared with us the vision God had given and prophesied over both of us the things God had been speaking. What was most interesting for us at this point was that in a vision Jim had seen God slap the United States of America. He had left the imprint of his hand upon the north-east and that imprint was the Finger Lakes region. God was going to 'dig a well of renewal' and we were to be a part of that. It confirmed for us the call we had already received from God.

One of the most popular posters displayed in homes in Ithaca is a photograph taken from a spacecraft on a beautiful clear day. It shows the Finger Lakes stretching down from Lake Ontario, looking for all the world like some giant had indeed hit hard and left a hand-print. Remarkably, we discovered that it was a native American legend that the Great Spirit had struck the land and left his mark. Was it possible that a prophetic word given by a Christian minister in the late twentieth century had previously been given within a native culture centuries before?

The discovery propelled us into reading more of Native American lore, sharing with friends and trying to discover as much as we could of ways in which God had revealed himself long before the 'white man' made an entrance in up-state New York. Since then, we have been struck by the number of times we have found truth—revealed truth—in native American wisdom and stories.

To be sure, we found superstition and animism. In parts of the culture, and among some tribes, we found what amounted to pure barbarism. Yet we were astonished by the wisdom and insight which we found in the traditional stories of the first Americans. We are aware that there is a need of discernment. In Genesis 14 Abram encountered not just righteous Melchizedek but also sinful Bera from Sodom. From Melchizedek Abram received bread and wine; from Bera he would take nothing. In the culture of the Canaanites Abram found both God's revelation and human depravity. He challenged the error and affirmed the good. It's a lesson we desperately need to learn as we live in postmodern culture.

As we continued to read native American history, it grieved us that in ignorance our European forebears destroyed much of that impressive culture without first seeking to understand it or to find the presence of our Father within it. Significantly, all over the US and Canada, there is a movement among Christians to repent for the mistreatment of native Americans, often abused in Christ's name, and to rebuild bridges which were destroyed centuries ago.

Rediscovering the charismatic and mystical

Besides the idea of natural theology (general revelation) and the Scriptures (special revelation), there is a third tradition which complements the former two. It is the tradition we might want loosely to call 'charismatic' or 'mystical', though both terms are so loaded that they almost immediately become redundant! It is that part of revelation concerned with the more direct, inner and intuitive revelation of God, Spirit to spirit.

Indeed, both the letter of the Scripture and the wonders of creation are brought to life through the inner work of the Spirit of God.

Some readers will be way ahead of us in this. Looking back on our lives as Christians we have been, like many in the evangelical churches, somewhat 'bookish' Christians. Our tradition has been to look for God, more or less exclusively, in his revealed words in the Bible and then in books about the Bible. Over the years, in charismatic renewal, we have learnt that God communicates directly to people's hearts; a kind of inner sensing of his presence and communication. In some respects, this has not been easy for us. We have been open to the prophetic and yet our experience of it, if truth be told, has been somewhat limited. Often, faith in God has been something of a 'wordy', conceptual thing. Furthermore, neither of us is, by temperament, a 'concrete' thinker. We operate most easily with ideas, propositions and theories. In pastoral ministry, when people shared 'pictures from God', we politely and genuinely thanked them, but were often unsure what to do with them. In this intense time of spiritual renewal, God is accelerating the learning curve for many of us. It will mean entering a new paradigm in our walk with God. It will also mean moving away from some of the things we have found most comfortable.

What we want to suggest and explore is that the heart of following Jesus Christ is to know this inner communication from God—Spirit to spirit—and that we are to develop a lifestyle in which we clearly hear him speak to us. It will include the Scriptures a great deal. But it will also include an awareness of the world around us, people, circumstances and situations. Through all of it our Father in heaven desires to enter into a deeper relationship with us.

Paul prayed for the Ephesians that they might have a 'spirit of wisdom and revelation in the full knowledge of him'. It is that which we are concerned with. Simply having the Bible does not guarantee revelation from God. Revelation only completes its purpose when it is received. The beautiful work of art may be finished, framed and displayed but until someone looks at the masterpiece and perceives its beauty and its greatness, the picture is not fulfilled. In many ways, it is the tragedy of great works of art being purchased as an investment, locked away in a vault and never being seen by human eyes. Paintings are designed to be looked at, considered and ought to make an impact on the beholder.

The Scriptures are like that. The Bible in its finished form is not unlike the great masterpiece painted by the Master Crafts-man. But there needs to be the interactive process of reader and text for the Bible's purpose to be fulfilled. However, because it deals with God—invisible, holy, infinite spirit—there is a need of inner, spiritual revelation in the process of reading and understanding. Even with the Bible, without the inner revelation of Spirit to spirit we will not have the revelation of God.

CHAPTER 4

SNIPPETS FROM HISTORY

From dynamic, inner faith to rationalism

In a pause during worship, Jenny hesitatingly and with some uncertainty in her voice says, 'I believe the Lord has a word for someone here today. He wants to encourage you, that in your despair he has not forgotten you. He loves you . . .'. Jenny's voice trails off and she begins quietly to weep, as if she is feeling in herself what God is feeling for some needy person in the congregation. If you were to ask Jenny after the meeting, 'How do you know it was God?' chances are she would answer something like this: 'I don't know. I just *knew* I felt it. It was a strong impression. I just had to say it.' Jenny is living in the experienced reality of God communicating his love and grace to her and through her to others.

Since earliest times there has been something of a debate about whether Christianity is concerned with the rational or the mystical. Is it something to be understood in the mind or experienced in the heart/spirit? In general, emphasis has been placed on the former. In fact, experiences are more often than not looked upon with some suspicion.

However, the New Testament holds both understanding and experience together. There is, without any doubt, a great deal of teaching, particularly in Paul's letters, which demonstrate for us what a reasoned orthodoxy looks like. Indeed, much of his writing was to correct errors which had crept into the church following bad teaching.

But there is also a great deal of the mystical: 'Christ in you the hope of glory' (Colossians 1:27); his 'Spirit which lives in us' (Romans 8:11); the 'Spirit witnessing with our spirit' (Romans 8:16); 'the anointing you have' (1 John 2:27), etc. It's also true that for the first Christians experience came before knowledge. They felt the power of the Spirit before they could ever understand the teaching about the Spirit. They were born again before they had a doctrine of regeneration. They began to walk in the Spirit's giftings before Paul gave them a list. They knew the indwelling of Jesus before the teachings about his indwelling were formulated.

Generally speaking, it's easier to deal with the doctrinal, rational, orthodoxy type questions than the mystical, experiential, orthopraxy type, and so the church has spent a great deal of time and mental effort in ensuring the correctness of its teaching. (Try wading through the church fathers' debates about the person of Christ in the fourth century, or the puritans wrestling with the Westminster Confession in the seventeenth and you will see what we mean.)

The trouble is, true Christianity will never allow itself to be merely about rationality. It is more than just mind. The God of the Bible, the Father of our Lord and Saviour Jesus Christ, is not merely a Big Mind communicating ideas and thoughts to other little minds. God is Spirit touching the human spirit in profound ways. God is personal relating to human persons in every aspect of what personality is. Communion with God necessarily involves mind, but also includes feeling, intuition, conscience and perception.

According to the New Testament, the indwelling Holy Spirit renews the mind (Romans 12:2) but also overwhelms the heart with joy (Romans 15:13), communicates peace to the soul (Philippians 4:7), reveals the divine glory which words cannot express (1 Peter 1:8), cries and groans from deep within (Romans 8:26), and enables a truly personal relationship with Abba, Father (Galatians 4:6). It amounts to an encounter with the divine, not so much in irrational ways but in trans-rational ways.

The seventeenth century in England produced rapid social and religious changes. The Reformation had become deeply rooted in the life of the nation and, freed from the medieval ideas of the unitarity of religion and culture, people began to develop a taste for religious freedom. The seventeenth century was the century of dissent.

However, tolerance for dissenters did not come easily. Persecution for expressing a different religious opinion was still prevalent. For some it meant standing firm regardless of the consequences, even if that meant imprisonment (as it did famously for John Bunyan). Others looked across the recently traversed ocean to a new world which held out the possibility of a different kind of society. Thousands of English Christians made the journey in barely seaworthy vessels to the new colonies—Virginia, New England and Rhode Island– to worship God in ways they believed were true. Yet old habits die hard and the pilgrims took with them some of the less noble character traits of English Christianity.

Mrs Anne Hutchinson was one such Christian adventuress. She followed her pastor John Mather to Massachusetts in search of a new and godly society.[18] She listened to John Mather's preaching about the freedom of grace. A number of like-minded women gathered each week in Anne's home as they carefully studied the pastor's sermons. As time passed, they determined to live the Christian life by the Spirit and not the letter of the law. Her teaching was so strong that in the end between sixty and eighty gathered at her home each week.

Warning bells were sounded. Anne's beliefs sounded dangerous. What if everyone started believing that people are to live by the Spirit and not the letter of the law? Surely, anarchy would follow. There would be no way to control the people.

In the manner of the day, Mrs Hutchinson was called before the colony's leaders. She held her own in debate and showed from the Scriptures that the early church lived by the Spirit. In fact, she proved her orthodoxy to the satisfaction of the colony's elders. Then she made her unforgivable mistake. She suggested that the Holy Spirit communicated with her directly, *apart from the Scriptures*. She did not claim infallibility, nor that the direct communication with God was equal to Scripture as a means of doctrine. Nor did she 'throw out' the Bible. She, and those who gathered with her, loved the Scriptures. But they also discovered that the word without the Spirit can be deadly and not life-giving. It was, however, the final straw for the religious leaders of New England. Anne Hutchinson and those who believed the same as her were banished from the Massachusetts colony. They settled later in the colony of New York where there was more toleration. Sadly, some years later Anne Hutchinson had a severely deformed baby. Her troubles came to a head when she and sixteen family members were killed in an Indian attack. In Massachusetts, wise old heads nodded in agreement that God himself had judged a heretic. Not a few whispered about the possibility of witchcraft.

New England Christianity found it difficult to deal with the mystical-prophetic side of the faith.

Here comes the caution

It is in these areas of the mystical and prophetic that caution is often expressed. There are many reasons for this. When the mystical is emphasised, following Jesus becomes a very subjective matter. It involves *my* experience, *my* feelings, and *my* intuition. And that is very difficult to either quantify or argue against. Every minister will have had the experience of some dear soul approaching after a service with a statement that goes like this: 'Pastor, the Lord has told me . . .'. It may well be to try to convince the leader that the church is not following God in some way or other and that there need to be changes. Most pastors will, in their turn, kindly receive the 'word' and give it some consideration. Not infrequently, the response will be, 'Well, the Lord hasn't said that to me yet!'

Indeed, too many of those kinds of 'words' are a thin cloak for somebody's own agenda. This kind of manipulation has discouraged some church leaders who refuse to take the prophetic and mystical seriously. Bad experiences have caused many of God's shepherds to deal firmly with the mystical in the flock, seeing the intuitive element of the faith as only for the quacks and those just a little eccentric! Some will not allow any kind of direct experience of the Spirit to be seen as valid. Sadly, this even proves true for some charismatics. Having once embraced the revelatory experience and having been 'burned', all prophetic ministry is given up as a bad job. A charismatic form remains without the inner reality.

Christian faith is easier to administer when the more spiritual side of things gives way to rationalism. If the faith can be distilled to that which can be understood through rational means then we can know who is in the right and who is in the wrong.

The early church councils which sought to reduce the mysteries of the Trinity and the incarnation to manageable propositions fell into this centuries old trap. The councils were, of course, driven by the purest of motives: to be able to define in words what is and what is not true Christian faith. In many ways that has helped us. There is a more or less clear body of propositions which we accept as the orthodox Christian faith concerning the Trinity, the person and work of Christ, the Holy Spirit, etc, and that is all to the good. A problem arises in that, having reduced the mystery to a form of words, we think we now understand the mystery. A form of words is only ever an imperfect vehicle to convey another reality. Just because someone says that they believe that Jesus Christ is God's Son does not mean that they truly understand all that they affirm. Nor does it mean that they have entered into the experience of the truth which they state. To reduce Christianity to a form of words is to take the heart from the faith. Words are only ever a vehicle carrying us to inner truth: guideposts pointing beyond themselves to other realities.

The tendency to try to reduce God to manageable words has been intensified in the centuries following the Enlightenment. Scholars began to doubt whether thinking people could truly believe the miraculous and experiential elements in the Bible. In a long process, which by the middle of this century became known as 'de-mythologising', Christianity became for many merely something to think about. The faith was reduced to that which an educated layperson could reasonably be expected to believe in. Of course, evangelicals firmly resisted the modernising tendencies of the liberal wing of the church. Great preachers, like Baptist C.H. Spurgeon (1834–92), even left their denominations because of it.

But still, the battle waged in fourth or twentieth centuries has often been related to the cognitive elements of what true Christianity is. We are sure that the battle for the mind is a necessary one. But the battle for the heart and spirit has largely gone unnoticed. Indeed, where some lone voice has been raised which suggests discipleship is a direct and immediate revelation and relationship with God, more often than not they have been declaimed as a heretic! The church has found it hard to deal with the experiential, often dismissively labelling it as the 'mystical' or the 'pietistic'. Of course, when something is labelled in this way it's easy to marginalise it. The mystical becomes just for those people with a particular bent—those on the fringes. The rest of us can live with a non-experiential, dry kind of faith. We believe it is time for the experiential heart of following Jesus to return to centre stage.

The Maid of Orléans

Childhood memories of Joan of Arc picture a dainty figure replete with shining battle armour and a round medieval knight's helmet carrying high a banner—the archetypal girl warrior. And warrior she was. But she was also a Christian girl who had a profound experience of God through dream and vision which the church of her day could not deal with.

Joan was born to a moderately wealthy yet simple family—her father was the local tax collector. By all accounts she was a pious girl who loved to pray when she heard the sound of the church bells ringing in her native village of Momremy in the north-eastern part of France. Indeed, it was at the sound of the church bell, as she was working in her parents' garden, that Joan had her first angelic visitation when she was just thirteen years old. She continued to live with direct revelation from God and by the age of seventeen took her destiny as the young girl, spoken of long before in prophecy, who would save the king of France. Stories about Joan multiplied. Some said she was a healer. Some that she was clairvoyant and could see into the future. The more bizarre stories did not help when it came to her later trial and execution for witchcraft.

Piecing the story of Joan of Arc into a whole is difficult.[19] The story is told with either the embellishment of fable or with the discrediting of the establishment. In an age of rampant superstition it is more than likely that some of the stories about Joan were the product of fertile imagination. We might want to discredit them all were it not for Joan's own testimony. Though Joan was tried for many serious sins (wearing men's clothing, being involved in superstition and not being taught the true Catholic faith, etc.), the most damning was that she had, herself, a direct communication with God which put her above the authority of the church. In her trial it became quite clear that she believed that she was led by revelation from God. That revelation at times came in what we would now term 'the word of knowledge'. She lived prophetically and was clearly very close to God. When faced with superstition or the adulation of the crowds she would shun it. When brought before the duplicity and cunning of the church-state establishment she answered with an honesty and simplicity which amazed even her detractors.

Like many others in the history of the church, it might be that the truth lies in the simple fact that Joan was a Christian who lived in the immediacy of a relationship with God, in which she knew his direct and personal communication—prophetic lifestyle—which the religion of her day did not know how to deal with.

The Anabaptists

Joan of Arc may have been something of a lone voice in France in the fifteenth century. Less than a hundred years later, in the aftermath of the European Reformation, there is the testimony of many who believed that true Christianity was about a deep relationship with God which was direct and personal.

Like Joan, the Anabaptists were not truly understood in their own day. Until comparatively recently the only view of the 'radical sects' we had was that they were the heretics of the Reformation. Trouble makers and anarchists, visionaries and polygamists, the Anabaptists were the marginal fringe of the great work of God through Luther and Calvin.

But we have come to understand them differently. Undoubtedly, the Anabaptists were not one unified body of Christians and there were clearly some excesses in the name of freedom. Yet many of the things we cherish dearly—religious freedom, the separation of church and state, the idea of the church as a freely gathered community of believers, the fact that we can all read the Bible for ourselves without either priest or pastor to be our divine interpreters, the gifting of women as well as men—were first proclaimed from the radical groups of the Reformation period.

Perhaps one of their greatest insights was that Christianity is about personal communication with God. In their day, they were considered to be too spiritual and it was a common criticism that the Anabaptists believed in revelation apart from the Bible. And they surely did! But the Anabaptists were also quick to point out that the immediate revelation God gave was never in contradiction to the written revelation of the Bible. The two belonged together. It was sometimes referred to as 'the inner and the outer word'[20] the inner word corresponding to the revelation of the Spirit and the outer to the revelation of the Bible. But there needed to be the inner revelation. For this reason the radical groups were less likely to produce a written statement of their beliefs. Merely to have a 'confession of faith' or creed did not of itself guarantee anything. The immediate experience of Christ by each believer personally, as the action of the Holy Spirit, was closer to the heart of their understanding.

At the time this emphasis was considered by both Protestant and Catholic churches to be too dangerous. It was one of the reasons the radical groups were persecuted and many of them executed. Policing the inner word is next to impossible if the issue is how to control others! How do you control those who repeatedly say they hear directly from God and not from you (if you are a leader of the church)?

We do, however, need to be aware of real dangers present when emphasis is placed on the inner life. Where there is no check on things (through the Scriptures or accountability between people) prophecy and 'visions' can get out of hand. On the extreme end of the radical groups, when prophecy went unrestrained and untempered by a consideration of the Scriptures it produced all kinds of oddities. Predictions of the end of the world were frequent in the Europe of the mid-sixteenth century. Some also had 'revelation' that because the end was near, the normal rules controlling sexual behaviour were no longer required. In some sects common relationships were established and sexual licence reigned. Others armed themselves against coming persecution. The most famous of these disastrous turns occurred in Münster in Westphalia in 1535 when a group of radicals, under misapplied prophetic words, declared Münster to be the New Jerusalem. The resultant moral anarchy produced a hefty backlash from the establishment and much blood was shed in the recapture of the city. The cages which contained the displayed corpses of the Anabaptist leaders are still hung on the church tower of St Lambert's. Let that be a warning to those of us who want to walk in prophetic lifestyle today!

The problem with the excesses of Münster is that the episode overshadows all the good things recovered by the radicals in post-Reformation Europe. It was long held that any emphasis on immediate revelation, visions or prophecy would end up like Münster. Fortunately, that is not true. Many believers of traditions as diverse as Anglicans and House Churches today look to the Anabaptists for spiritual roots.

What about the Quakers!

Similar eruptions to that in Europe took place just about a hundred years later in England. The breakdown of the religious establishment in the mid-seventeenth century gave an impetus to religious freedom. Like new wine, freedom is heady stuff! Many became 'seekers' and washed their hands of the outward forms of religion, preferring instead to meditate for themselves upon the Scriptures and to seek an inner experience of God. Perhaps the most famous seeker of all is George Fox (1624–91) who is looked to as the founder of the Society of Friends. Amid the plethora of clamouring voices, Fox proclaimed a message which was at once simple yet profound. True Christianity lies with a discovery of the inner light. Mere outward sacramentalism is worthless and does not lead towards true godliness.

Some of Fox's habits seem quaint—never taking off his hat, addressing everyone by the pronouns 'Thee' or 'Thou', his publicly entering churches (steeple houses, he called them) to denounce the preacher, to name but a few. Some of the prophetic actions of his followers might also raise an eyebrow or two. James Naylor, one of Fox's converts, for example, allowed followers to worship him as the Son of God upon entering Bristol in 1656.

However, the enduring nature of the movement points away from the occasional excesses and towards the profundity at the heart of Fox's message. It is the place of every follower of Christ to find the 'inner light' for themselves. God will actually teach his children by being 'Abba', guiding his children through his indwelling Spirit, rather than through outward legalism.

Bishop Brooke Foss Wescott said of George Fox:

Fox judged truly that the new Protestant scholasticism had not reached to the heart of things in any image of past experience, or in any printed book however sacred: that academic learning was not in itself an adequate passport to the Christian ministry; that the words of God should not supersede the Word of God. He realised, as few men have ever realised, that we are placed under the dispensation of the Spirit: that the power from on high with which the risen Christ promised to endue His People was no exceptional or transitory gift, but an Eternal Presence, an unfailing spring of energy, answering to new wants and new labours. He felt that the Spirit which had guided the fathers was waiting still to lead forward their children: that He who spoke through men of old was not withdrawn from the world like the gods of Epicurus, but ready in all ages to enter into holy souls and make them friends of God and prophets.[21]

Jeanne Guyon

The number of those who have walked a truly prophetic life-style in the history of the church forms a small but distinguished company. In nearly all instances they had few friends within the established church. We realise that our brief dip into history has been haphazard, incomplete and very selective. We wanted simply to unfurl a flag pointing to some of those who have taken the inner way of communion with God in which they moved beyond mere religion into a true experience of communication with the Father. We include just one more snap-shot.

Jeanne Guyon was born in 1648 in the town of Montargis, some fifty miles south of Paris. She was baptised and raised in the Roman Catholic Church and never sought any other spiritual home. She had a fairly unremarkable childhood, other than being married at the tender age of sixteen. In 1668 she experienced God in a personal way for the first time and immediately gave herself to God to be his servant. She began a life of closely walking with God, seeing his revelation in dreams and through the rediscovery that true Christianity is about the inner life. In 1685, after many years of seeking God, Madame Guyon published her short book on the *Method of Prayer*.[23] She began to influence the many people she had contact with and her writings spread to many parts of France. She was misunderstood by the religious authorities of her day: her teachings were considered heretical and dangerous. The very suggestion that a simple, uneducated woman might have some precious insights from God to share with her generation was considered anathema. Jeanne Guyon faced hostilities first in the form of accusation (Surely she was a witch? Didn't she have a mysterious hold over her followers?), then through examination and judgement, followed by the public burning of her writings. Finally, she was imprisoned a number of times. First, in 1688 for ten months and then in 1695 at Vincennes with an eventual transfer to the infamous Bastille for four years from 1698 to 1702. Her crime? She claimed that she had entered into a relationship of perfect love with God and that God communicated directly with her without mediation of church or priest.[23]

In truth, we probably would not want to suggest that Anne Hutchinson, Joan of Arc, the Anabaptists, the Quakers or Jeanne Guyon were flawless examples of Christianity. We might want to point out errors and excesses in all these imperfect followers of Jesus Christ. However, we want to highlight them to make two simple observations. First, there have been those who have lived prophetically. They have dared to live in the 'now' of God's presence, to feel the gentle breeze of the Holy Spirit, to allow him to move them as he saw fit and to do so even when it took them beyond that which was accepted as normal in the church of their day.

Secondly, it seems that whenever God has allowed some of his children to have deeper spiritual and mystical insights into the faith, they have often been misunderstood and marginalised. Thankfully, in recent years there has been a tendency to rehabilitate these misconstrued saints and we are beginning to learn from their different experiences of God. We are being enriched by their pilgrimages. Is it too much to ask that we might find the same courage from God within ourselves to walk the same way?

CHAPTER 5

DREAMS AND VISIONS

Dreams and visions were a very important part of the life of the Celtic church. They were not something rare or for special occasions, but a normal, everyday part of life. Dreams were the way the creator communicated with his creation. Sometimes, interpretation was left to others.

> Ciaran went to the island of Aran to commune with Enda. Both of them saw the same vision of a great fruitful tree growing beside a stream in the middle of Ireland. This tree protected the entire island, its fruit crossed the sea that surrounded Ireland, and the birds of the world came to carry off some of the fruit.
>
> Ciaran turned to Enda and told him what he had seen. Enda said to him:
>
> 'The great tree you saw is you, Ciaran, for you are great in the eyes of God and of all humankind. All of Ireland will be sheltered by the grace that is in you, and many people will be fed by your fasting and prayers. Go in the name of God to the centre of Ireland and found your church on the banks of a stream.'[24]

Samthann was a Celtic saint who was given charge over a monastery through a vision. The revelation was given to

Funecha, who was the foundress of the monastery at Clonbro-ney. In her dream, Funecha saw Samthann as a spark of fire which grew to a great flame and burnt over all the monastery. Funecha interpreted it as Samthann burning with the Holy Spirit, and that through her the monastery would be alight with power and miracles. Samthann was made Abbess of the monastery.

Often the dreams and visions foretold the future. Sanctus (the father of David) had a dream in which an angel appeared to him and said:

> 'Tomorrow you will awake and go hunting. You will kill a stag near a river, and in that place you will find three gifts, namely the stag you will pursue, a fish and a hive of bees. Now of these three, you will set aside the honeycomb and a portion of the fish and of the stag. These you will send to Maucannus's monastery, there to be preserved for a son who will be born of you.'

> These three gifts overshadowed David's life. The honeycomb declared his wisdom, for just as honey lies embedded in wax, so he perceived the spiritual meaning within a literal statement. The fish proclaimed his abstinence, for as the fish lives by water, so David rejected wine, fermented liquor and everything intoxicat-ing. The stag signified his power over the ancient serpent. For as the stag, after feeding on the snakes it has destroyed, longs for a spring of water, so David selected his own well of life with a ceaseless flow of tears.[25]

To our rationalistic mindset, some of the Celtic stories, though delightful in themselves, raise many questions. Is the story true? Do stags kill snakes *really*? However, to raise these kinds of questions is to miss the point of the story and to impose a particular world-view—that of post-Enlightenment scientific rationalism upon a story told in a different context. It is part of the poverty of our culture that we can only perceive truth as that which can be scientifically measured and demonstrated. If the Celtic stories tell us anything at all, it is that there is a different way of living, of perceiving and of enjoying the life God has given us. We are beginning to learn that God places great value on the creative use of the imagination and the interaction of the Holy Spirit. In prophetic lifestyle we will be open to dreams and visions—and to God for wisdom in interpreting them.

Snakes in the grass

'By the way,' Jane said as we drove to the shopping centre in our ubiquitous Ford Taurus station wagon, 'Rebekah had a strange dream last night.'

We had begun to learn that dreams have their place in the prophetic lifestyle.

'She said she saw two green snakes sitting on the doorstep. They were half as thick as she is and longer.'

What a snake looks like 'sitting' we can only imagine. We have found that dreams, particularly from children, are often graphic and told in a way which adults find difficulty in visualising.

Jane continued, 'Rebekah was frightened and you told her not to worry because snakes don't come in houses. But they came into the house and Rebekah ran up stairs. Then you assured her not to worry because snakes couldn't climb stairs. But they did! And then Rebekah woke up.'

'What did I do a silly thing like that for?' Andy mused, 'Still, it may be a warning of some kind or other. Better seek the Lord.'

Some time later, when Andy had a time of prayer, he shared the whole affair with the Lord. Through prayer, meditation and asking for God's guidance a number of things became clear.

The presence of snakes in the dream was ominous. We had become aware that snakes in visions and dreams (and in real life!) can be a sign of the enemy's working. Jesus had said as much when he told his disciples:

> I watched Satan fall from heaven like a flash of lightning. See, I have given you authority to tread on snakes and scorpions, and over all the power of the enemy; and nothing will hurt you. Nevertheless, do not rejoice at this, that the spirits submit to you, but rejoice that your names are written in heaven.
>
> Luke 10:18–20

In the passage Jesus uses the term 'snakes and scorpions' as a metaphor for 'the power of the enemy' and the 'spirits' which the disciples were able to cast out. Since Eden, references to snakes more often than not have the meaning of Satan or evil spirits.

We had experienced a similar situation some months before Rebekah's dreams. On arriving in the USA, we were to live temporarily at a house in the country for a week or two. It was a beautiful July day and we opened the car doors with some relief having driven the best part of six hours. Jane had taken a few steps away from the car and for some reason looked down to the ground. Moving slowly between her feet there was a snake of some two or three feet in length. She screamed and ran for cover! We learned later that the snakes native to New York State are not poisonous. Nevertheless, it was an unnerving experience.

The following morning Jane went out of the back door to hang out some washing on the line—somewhat nervously it must be said! Astonishingly, as she looked at the ground, there was an even larger snake only a few inches from her feet. Andy heard the scream from round the front of the house.

Friends who have lived up-State for many years told us that they had never seen any snakes, and certainly not at the times of day we did. We prayed about the matter, shared it with some wise friends and concluded that through a visible and physical demonstration God was telling us that there would be some 'serpent' activity just around the corner. Sure enough, within a few days we were engulfed in strong spiritual warfare that pushed us to the limits of our faith and to the point of total reliance upon God.

We brought all of those thoughts and experiences to Rebekah's dream of the two snakes. As Andy pondered the dream, seeking God's interpretation, it became clear that he himself had opened the door in the dream. Now that was unnerving. We know that none of us is beyond failing a temptation, but was God actually saying that Andy was in danger of opening a door within the family to the work of the enemy? It seemed so.

Another important element was that in the dream there was clearly deception. 'Snakes don't climb stairs,' Andy had said confidently. Was there an area of deception Andy was under and through which he was in danger of allowing the enemy in? Andy prayed further, asking God to shed any light necessary where the warning of the dream might prove to be true. The Holy Spirit highlighted two particular areas which needed Andy's attention in his personal life. After due repentance Andy made a covenant with God to deal with those areas. In this way, through God's goodness in bringing revelation to a family member, the strategy of the enemy was confounded and victory won. With regard to Rebekah's dream, because of our knowledge of Scripture and based on our past experience and discernment, we decided not only was the dream from God but that it demanded some kind of action.

Revelation, interpretation, application

The snake incident provides a useful example of what to do with prophetic insights, whether they are brought to us by dream, vision, word of knowledge or some other means. It seems to us that three elements are always present and provide a process which we need to work through in being obedient to God's direction.

First, there is discernment of the revelation or action itself to determine whether we believe it is from God. We have given sufficient illustrations to demonstrate how revelation may be given. But there is the necessary process of discernment: is the revelation genuine? Not all which charismatically glistens is spiritual gold and we need to be able to distinguish what is significant. How we know when a dream or word is from God is a vital concern and more consideration is given to this in chapter 11 when we look at testing all things prophetic. If it's decided that a 'revelation' is not from God, then that is the end of the matter.

However, even when a vision is discerned to be of God it is only the beginning. It is important to ask, 'What do we do with this revelation?' Revelation is never an end in itself but always leads to other things.

In this regard, dealing with inspirational words, events and visions is much the same as dealing with the Scriptures. Even though the revelation of the Scriptures is complete, there is a need to interpret what God has given us. Occasionally folk say something to the effect of 'All we need are the Scriptures. We don't need anyone to interpret them. We just take them as they are.' The sentiment is a good one and sounds somewhat similar to the Reformation principle of *sola scriptura*, scripture only. The principle the Reformers followed, however, was that scripture stands alone and above tradition. There is nothing else which approaches the Bible in inspiration and authority (and we are certainly not suggesting in any way that present prophetic words equal the Scripture). However, even given that formative principle, the revelation given us in the Bible needs to be interpreted. That is what all the Bible concordances, dictionaries and commentaries, biblical preaching and Bible study are all about. We need to interpret the revelation given us in the Scriptures to gain a better understanding of God's ways.

This leads us to the important subject of hermeneutics—the art and science of interpretation. Space forbids any realistic treatment of this fascinating area[26] but all serious Bible students know that interpretation is crucially important. If such care is needed with the Scriptures we must be equally diligent with the interpretation of revelatory gifts. A vision given in church on Sunday morning cannot be left to stand alone. When it is decided that it is a true revelatory gift from God we still need to interpret what God is saying. We want to suggest a few guidelines:

- Interpretation of revelations and prophecies must be in the light of the Scriptures. Any interpretation of a vision which runs contrary to the Scriptures cannot be allowed.
- Don't try to manufacture an interpretation. Wait upon the Spirit of God, seek him and listen to the inner voice of the Spirit.
- Seek out those who are mature in faith and who have some experience of understanding prophetic insights.

- If an interpretation is not immediately given, the prophecy need not be rejected but rather held until God's time is perceived. Doubtless, there are prophecies in the Scriptures for which we are still waiting God's time for interpretation.
- It is often not the receiver of the revelation who interprets. In fact, it is better if the interpretation is left to the body of believers who can seek God and discern together. This is also a safeguard against those who bring a 'revelation' and seek to bring an interpretation which is really their own agenda.

There is a third step which follows interpretation and that is application. God's revelation is always towards something. To hear and not to do is never satisfactory. After revelation comes interpretation. It may be a point of obedience. It may be a warning to us which we need to take special note of. More often than not revelatory gifting leads towards prayer. God reveals something so that we can take that revelation back to him in intercession.

The three stages in the process of receiving prophetic revelation may be phrased in the form of questions:

- Is this from God?
- If it is, what does it mean?
- If that is the meaning, what are we to do about it?

Interpreters of dreams . . . Joseph

Joseph provides an interesting example of what not to do with prophetic revelation! In Genesis 37, as a young man of seventeen, Joseph is given insights from God through dreams. The dreams are very vivid, the interpretation is clear, but Joseph mishandles the gift and causes a lot of heartache.

Jacob loved Joseph more than all his other children. The trouble was that Joseph knew it and, unwisely, Jacob allowed his other sons to know it too. Joseph in his turn played up to his father at the expense of his brothers. He became Jacob's 'spy'. The straw that broke the collective back of the clan came when Jacob singled Joseph out for special treatment in the gift of a beautiful coat. Resentment built within the family— clearly trouble was brewing! Resentment turned to hatred and the brothers could not find a civil word to say to Joseph.

Then Joseph had a dream. The brothers' sheaves bowed down to the tall standing sheaf of Joseph. The implication was clear. Everyone got the message. The brothers were to be in submission to Joseph. Dreams were not to be taken lightly and the interpretation of the dream was clear to all concerned. Perhaps if Joseph had been a decent sort of brother the implication would not have been so unpalatable. But they didn't like him to start with and now there was more fuel for their hatred and bitterness.

Joseph was a slow learner. He had another dream in which the sun, moon and eleven stars bowed down to him. He told dad and mum. They were as cross as the brothers. Coming from the young seventeen-year-old it sounded like mere impertinence.

There was no problem with the dreams. God gave them. There was no difficulty over the interpretation, for in this instance the symbolism of the dreams was fairly transparent. Joseph's trouble came with the application of his insights. It would seem most likely that the dreams were for Joseph's own insights. God was allowing him to see the great plan he had in store: perhaps for Joseph to hold and pray about; perhaps to help focus the direction of his life. Joseph mishandled the visions. We know, of course, that God turned the circumstances around to Joseph's good. There is the wonderful verse towards the end of the story: 'Even though you intended to do harm to me, God intended it for good, in order to preserve a numerous people, as he is doing today' (Genesis 50:20).

It does not, however, nullify the fact that Joseph wrongly used the visions he had both to injure his family and ultimately to cause himself a great deal of trouble. Clearly, with prophetic lifestyle we need a lot of spiritual wisdom!

Interpreters of dreams . . . Daniel

In Daniel's day interpreting dreams was a serious business. Cautious fellow that he was, King Nebuchadnezzar wanted both the dream and the interpretation to be given. Give the wrong interpretation and according to the great, but doubting, king, 'If you do not tell me both the dream and the interpretation, you will be torn limb from limb, and your houses shall be laid in ruins' (Daniel 2:5).

Such a decree sharpens the mind and gives the would-be prophetic interpreter a little more focus! Later, when in a rage, the king decided that all the 'wise men of Babylon' be killed, Daniel answered with 'prudence and discretion' (Daniel 2:14). His demeanour was in contrast to the young Joseph who was somewhat reckless with his revelatory insights. Daniel and his companions sought God. The dream and interpretation are given but not through any great wisdom on Daniel's part. Dream and interpretation come from God. When brought before the king Daniel takes the place of humility and tells the king that no 'wise men, enchanters, magicians or diviners' could do what the king asked. However, 'there is a God in heaven who reveals mysteries' (Daniel 2:28). It shows us clearly that to adopt a prophetic lifestyle, humility is not just a desirable virtue but a necessary prerequisite.

Furthermore, Daniel did not profit from the great gift God had given him. In Chapter 5 the king promises great wealth and position to Daniel if he interprets visions correctly. Daniel for his part replies that the king can keep his riches! God's gifts are not to be marketed. It is a clear example for those with a prophetic ministry today.

On another occasion the interpretation of a dream was found to be quite terrifying. However, Daniel sought the interpretation regardless of the consequences. He concludes his narrative, 'As for me, Daniel, my thoughts greatly terrified me, and my face turned pale; but I kept the matter in my mind' (Daniel 7:28). Where Joseph told all, Daniel held the dream and interpretation to himself. There would be a time to to reveal God's secret, but not yet. Truly wisdom is needed.

Dreams and visions in the New Testament

As we began to look into the whole area of dreams and visions, we were struck that revelatory events were a perfectly normal part of New Testament church life. It's not just that they are there, but that visions and dreams are accepted as a normal and ordinary part of what it means to follow Jesus.

In the narratives surrounding the birth of Jesus, dreams are a frequent occurrence. Zechariah sees the angel in the temple and is struck dumb (Luke 1:11ff). The angel appears to Joseph in a dream (Matthew 1:20). The angel appears to Mary to announce the purpose of God (Luke 1:28), and the angels appear to the shepherds in the fields (Luke 2:9). We want to look now only at the visit of the Magi which reveals the warning nature of dreams.

From the brief account of the 'wise men' we can probably discern that they lived what we call a prophetic lifestyle. They had observed a particular star in which they had seen a significance communication of God. It may well have been a natural phenomenon, but they perceived in it God's voice speaking of the rising of a new king. They visited the king's palace in search of the new king who had been born. Of course, he was not there and they continued their prophetic pilgrimage until they found the child Jesus in Bethlehem.

Having worshipped him they are again faced with the voice of God—this time in a dream warning them not to return to Herod. They leave and return home by a different route. Immediately after their departure, Joseph himself has a dream in which the angel warns of Herod's hatred of the child and his desire to kill Jesus.

Twice in the space of a couple of verses dreams are used as warnings. It may well be that if we choose to take notice of our dreams, we too may find our Father communicating with us to warn us of impending situations.

While reading the book of Acts, we were impressed with the sense that here was a church that lived in the immediacy of God's presence. The apostles expected God's continual revelation to them. Often this revelation came in the form of dreams and visions. Stephen was given a vision of heaven as he faced martyrdom: '"Look", he said, "I see the heavens opened and the Son of Man standing at the right hand of God"' (Acts 7:56).

Ananias had a vision telling him to go and find Saul and lay hands on him so he would regain his sight. Furthermore Saul was to become a chosen instrument to take God's revelation to the gentiles. And Ananias went! Surely he must have gone in fear and trembling, being aware of Saul's reputation for persecuting the Christians, but to Ananias the most important thing was being obedient to the vision he had received.

Similarly, Peter was given the vision where he saw a large sheet from heaven coming down filled with all sorts of beasts that were traditionally unclean for him to eat. Visions were accepted as one of the ways that God communicates. Though Peter was unsure of the vision at first, it was not the idea of vision or trance which gave pause for reflection but the content of the vision. That God would speak through a dream or a vision or in a trance was an accepted part of Christian prophetic lifestyle.

Some people are more prone to receiving visions and having dreams than others. In part, it is a temperamental thing. What is a natural part of life often becomes intensified and used by God when someone commits their life to Christ. Pam is one such 'dreamer'. Ever since she was a little girl, she remembers having dreams which often came true. Her dreams were often of good things and many times having had a dream she would relive it shortly afterwards in her day-to-day life.

One series of dreams remains very vivid for they all concerned an event which was to have a profound effect on her life. Pam's husband David was killed in a car accident just two months after she had become a Christian. Dealing with such tragedy is immensely hard, but Pam was prepared by God through dreams. On three occasions she had the same dream in which her husband was killed. On the night of his death, Pam was sitting on the settee at home and actually heard a car accident. She told us that it was as if she was lifted off the settee and heard the Lord say, 'It's David—he's dead.' None of her neighbours heard any accident and it was confirmed that

David had actually died at the moment Pam heard the accident. It's not the kind of dream any of us would like to experience, let alone the reality which followed, but it demonstrates to us the validity of dreams and the way God will use them. Pam is sure that if she had not been warned in the series of dreams she would have taken David's death even harder. In God's mercy he had allowed her time to prepare.

Speaking of death is uncomfortable in our culture. The Celtic saints were not as uneasy. There were a number of times when God prophetically revealed the time of a saint's death. Boisil was Cuthbert's mentor, soul friend, prophet and a very holy man. In his prophetic walk God revealed to him that he would shortly leave this life. In preparation for his death Boisil shared with Cuthbert that he only had one week to live. The warning gave Cuthbert and Boisil the opportunity to spend a happy week together studying John's Gospel. Boisil's commentary was in seven parts and they decided to read one commentary each day. They studied together concentrating on the simple things of faith working by love. On the seventh day as they finished Boisil fell ill and shortly afterwards died. In God's goodness he had given time for both Boisil and Cuthbert to prepare for his homecoming.

CHAPTER 6

PARABLES AND PROPHETIC STORY-TELLING

'Do you remember when we climbed that hill in Scotland? You know, the one in the pine trees where Dad and Rebekah made up that song and sang it for hours!' Ben enthused one afternoon.

'That was a great holiday,' Jane remembered with a smile. 'What about those two stags we saw with the huge antlers, just off the side of the road?'

'And that lovely meal we had in that pub overlooking the loch,' Andy continued.

Our conversation bubbled on for a while as we told and retold and reminisced about a great family holiday. The retelling of the story brought all kinds of happy memories and good feelings for each of us. Story telling is a wonderful part of being in a relationship.

Celtic Christians were great story-tellers. In pre-literary culture, telling stories, passing on tales from generation to generation, was a powerful educational tool.

Psalm 78 is one of many Psalms which retell the story of

God's dealing with Israel. Many of the Psalms are like that. It begins, 'Give ear, O my people, to my teaching . . .' and proceeds to recount a story. It is a story which tells of God's goodness and mercy in bearing with a people who more often than not turned away from him. It speaks of his continued giving of sustenance and care even when people are in rebellion against him. Even in his anger he answers them only with compassion. Strictly speaking there are here no doctrines or propositions about God but rather the dramatic telling of a story in which God moves. The narrative demonstrates what God is like rather than describing in an abstract or conceptual way who he is.

In our society we have been discovering recently that story is both a powerful means of communication and something which shapes the people we are. For a long time in the enlightened West, certainly in theology and philosophy, there was a move away from the simplicity of the concrete and visual 'telling of a story' to the more conceptual, abstract and analytical. Stories were considered something from pre-enlightened times, relics from before the dawn of reason, something for children which we leave behind when we mature. Grown-ups don't tell stories. They think and analyse and conceptualise. One of the effects of this was to put theology and philosophy out of the reach of ordinary people.

However, in recent years there has been a shift in theology and philosophy towards narrative theology and narrative ethics, in which stories are being seen again as that which shape culture and have a profound effect upon our lives.

The philosopher Alasdair MacIntyre says, 'It is because we all live out narratives in our lives and because we understand our own lives in terms of narratives that we live out that the form of narrative is appropriate for understanding the actions of others.'[27]

People do not live in an abstract world of concepts and ideas. Our lives have a certain shape to them. There is a beginning, a middle and an end. There are tragedies, victories, boring times, sad times and happy times. And all of it weaves together as the story of our lives.

Of course, we have known this all along. Christians have always been powerfully affected by the stories of Israel and Jesus. We have always realised the benefit of telling the stories to our children. When our boys were small and we came to the nightly ritual of the story we would tell them over and over again the stories of Daniel, of Samson, of Noah and the Ark and Peter and John in the Acts. They never seemed to tire of them. When Jane was a young child her father would make up stories about the 'Badger Family'—Billy, Brock and Baby and Mr and Mrs Badger. When our children were small, we too continued the tradition. The simple little stories fired the imagination and (in the nature of the telling) spoke to the children about their own lives. The nightly narrative of the badgers helped them make sense of the things which happened to them. When friends betrayed their budding friendships, the badgers too would face a similar difficulty. Stories help us with the realisation 'Yes, it was a bit like that for me too.'

For ourselves, we have loved to listen each year to the story of the birth of Jesus. In fact, we realised just how much we love the story and need to hear it when we found a culture in which it was being eradicated. Political correctness has its virtues and vices. Removing unnecessarily sexist or racist language is a good thing. But at times well-loved and important aspects of common culture are 'banned' to the detriment of most.

We had been looking forward to our first truly 'white

Christmas' in up-state New York where snow is almost guaranteed. We weren't disappointed. In the event snow began on 7th November and continued into the first week of May! Yet snow, making the countryside look like every scenic Christmas card we had ever received, did not make up for what we discovered had happened to Christmas. C.S. Lewis's awful possibility of 'always winter and never Christmas' from his Narnia chronicles is not too far from the truth of the secular society. Publicly, Christmas is banned! There can be no public nativity scenes. No carols are played in shops—Christmas ditties about snowmen (sorry snow-people!), and sleigh bells are OK, but nothing overtly Christian. Nowhere does it say 'Happy Christmas', only the bland 'Happy Holidays'. Even the local daily newspaper, in its TV section, merely announced the day as 25th December. It was simply business as usual. The Christmas story cannot be told in the state schools for fear of upsetting minorities who do not share the celebration of Christmas and the children do not engage in Christmas nativity plays. There are no school carol services. In our daughter Rebekah's school they read Charles Dickens' *A Christmas Carol* and had to write an essay about it without mentioning Christmas! We tried to get hold of a little colouring book of the Christmas story for some of the young children in our home church. There were none to be found.

It took us a while to realise it, but Christmas in parts of the USA has been secularised in ways we have not yet come to in the UK. Quite simply, we missed the story. We missed hearing it. We missed seeing any reference to it anywhere. The Christmas story has shaped us since we were little children and we have been used to its familiar ring each year. Without its retelling at Christmas our common culture is all the poorer. Stories shape us more than we think. We had thought that the idea of 'Christmas spirit' was a product of Victorian sentimentality. Now we believe that people are unconsciously yet powerfully effected by the telling and retelling of the birth of Jesus—peace on earth and goodwill to all.

Parable as prophetic story

Jesus, of course, used stories as one of the primary means of his teaching. His style was in distinct contrast to the lecturing style of Greek and Roman philosophy with its enormous complexities only understood by the initiated. We must also admit that Jesus' teaching style appears somewhat different to the stylised sermons and carefully practised oratory of most Christian preaching. His seems to be a more 'natural' and informal sharing with those close to him. Even his public declarations seemed more to do with telling short stories than delivering a well-reasoned and thoughtful 'three pointer'.

Matthew tells us that Jesus' teaching style had more authority than that of the religious scholars of his time (Matthew 7:29). Religious teaching, then as now, is often the citing of authorities: 'Rabbi so-and-so said this—but Rabbi so-and-so said that.' Jesus told stories which carried an impact and authority people were not used to hearing. In fact, Matthew goes so far as to say that when Jesus spoke to the crowds his sole teaching method was to speak 'in parables'.

Anyone who has studied the parables of Jesus will have come across an explanation of his using them in this way: Jesus taught using stories so everyone could understand. Parables were earthly stories with a heavenly meaning which everyone could grasp. Parables were illustrations so that what Jesus said was, 'It's a bit like this . . .' and told a story.

Pressing further, students of the parables find something a

little hard to deal with. In Matthew 13:10 Jesus is asked: 'Why do you speak to them in parables?'

We might expect him to reply to the effect that it's so people can understand more easily. His reply is somewhat different: 'The reason I speak to them in parables is that "seeing they do not perceive, and hearing they do not listen, nor do they understand."'

There is something of the enigmatic in the stories Jesus told. Mark makes it even more explicit.

> And he said to them, 'To you has been given the secret of the kingdom of God, but for those outside, everything comes in parables; in order that "they may indeed look, but not perceive, and may indeed listen, but not understand; so that they may not turn again and be forgiven."'
>
> (Mark 4:11–12)

The stories, it seems, are not a means of evangelising the outsiders but are for those who are already committed. Yet a difficulty remains, for the stories themselves are more or less simple stories of everyday events. How can people not understand them?

It might help to place alongside this teaching of Jesus what Paul says in 1 Corinthians 2:6–14—

> Yet among the mature we do speak wisdom, though it is not a wisdom of this age or of the rulers of this age, who are doomed to perish. But we speak God's wisdom, secret and hidden, which God decreed before the ages for our glory. None of the rulers of this age understood this; for if they had, they would not have crucified the Lord of glory. But, as it is written, 'What no eye has seen, nor ear heard, nor the human heart conceived, what God has prepared for those who love him'—these things God has revealed to us through the Spirit; for the Spirit searches everything, even the depths of God. For what human being knows what is truly human

except the human spirit that is within? So also no one compre-
hends what is truly God's except the Spirit of God. Now we have
received not the spirit of the world, but the Spirit that is from
God, so that we may understand the gifts bestowed on us by God.
And we speak of these things in words not taught by human
wisdom but taught by the Spirit, interpreting spiritual things to
those who are spiritual. Those who are unspiritual do not receive
the gifts of God's Spirit, for they are foolishness to them, and they
are unable to understand them because they are spiritually
discerned.

Placing Paul's teaching next to what Jesus says about his use
of parables helps us. Even the simple use of stories will not
help people understand who do not know the Spirit of God.
There is more to grasping spiritual truth than understanding
with the mind. God uses the simplicity of story to confound
the wise, for the story will only be truly understood when the
Spirit of God brings insight.

With this in mind we want to suggest that the stories Jesus
told were more than 'just stories'. If we recall the words of
Professor F.F. Bruce regarding prophecy as 'the declaration of
the mind of God in the power of the Spirit, with a special
bearing on the current situation', and apply that to the way
Jesus taught we might begin to gain an understanding of the
parable as a prophetic story. In this way we are looking at the
parables of Jesus, not so much as an illustration of truth (which
might be a natural exercise) but as the declaring of God's mind
in the power of the Spirit in *the form of story*. In other words the
form is story-telling, but the content is spiritual prophetic
declaration of the heart of God. And because it is a spiritual
exercise and not merely a rational or mental exercise there is a
need of the Spirit in the lives of the hearers.

This was clearly the case when Jesus told his stories. For

many people who listened there was no revelation of the heart of God. Jesus' teaching, it seems, confused them. His stories stirred up dark feelings and indignation in some people. They wanted to hear no more! Yet others, who in the telling of the stories also received spiritual revelation, were profoundly moved.

When Jesus spoke of living bread and eating his body and drinking his blood—very vivid word pictures—many couldn't receive it. John 6 tells the whole tragic incident. Even some of those who had wanted to be his followers drew back. His sayings were too hard. Peter, speaking for those who had received the Spirit's revelation answered, 'To whom shall we go. You have the words of eternal life.' The stories of Jesus had conveyed to those disciples life-giving revelation of the Father's heart.

Narnia and other children's (sic) stories

C.S. Lewis's Narnia series of books are for children, aren't they? Apparently not! We were amused to follow a discussion on the Internet by a group of philosophers from various universities who argued over the symbolic meaning of one of the characters in the books. 'Tash surely stands for the devil, Satan,' argued one. 'No, I think Tash stands for the god of a non-Christian religion,' argued another. The debate lasted for a number of days as letters were posted from around the world.

The truth is, C.S. Lewis had the remarkable facility of telling a good story. Good enough for children to read and enjoy and good enough for serious philosophers to argue over the interpretation of one of the subsidiary characters! Story speaks to young and old alike, to the simplicity of a child and the profundity of the theologian with varying amounts of sophistication—but always with impact.

We did feel, however, that our philosopher friends were barking up the wrong tree. There is probably no 'true interpretation' of Lewis in the sense of finding some definitive meaning. At various points in our lives, with our differing needs and mental/emotional states we all respond differently to the same story. But central to narrative is the way in which it may speak prophetically to us in deeper ways than propositional or philosophical truths.

The stories of Narnia always have an impact. To read of Aslan is to catch glimpses of the Lord. He is infinitely patient with his erring subjects, yet terrifying to his enemies. Those closest to him will often see him; those with doubts will look incredulously: 'Where's the lion?' His roar shakes the very foundations of the earth, yet he allows little girls to play with him, to run their fingers through his soft mane, to ride on his back and to find safety tucked under his huge paws as they sleep. When mistakes are made, one look at the lion's face brings deep conviction to the perpetrator, yet the lion himself makes no great affair of the sin and always offers grace and kindness. And when a little boy pleads for the life of his dying mother, huge great tears of sadness appear in the lion's eyes. With the 'eyes of the heart' opened wide, the stories of Narnia can be a deeply moving spiritual experience. The stories speak prophetically in all kinds of ways, not least about the inner life of faith in the interaction of Narnia and 'this world'.

Cutgate Baptist Church in Rochdale was our first 'student pastorate'. It was a small congregation of mostly elderly people—dear people who were used to teach pastoral principles to potential pastors. They endured a great deal! We still remember the profound impact of simply reading the whole crucifixion story one Good Friday at a communion service. The narrative was read without comment and the impact of the 'naked' story brought most of the thirty-plus congregation to tears. Each responded in a different way as the Spirit of God brought deep revelation of the love of God in Christ. The effect of the story was deeper than words could express. What doctrine had been imparted? It's difficult to say. Could the communicants express more clearly their understanding of the atonement? We doubt it. But the simple act of communion with the telling of the story of Jesus' suffering brought people into a realisation of God's immense love and sacrifice. It was not so much understood in the head as felt deeply in the heart.

A tale of two Oscar winners

Good contemporary stories are often told at the movies. In some Christian circles, having a night out at the cinema is frowned upon as somehow 'worldly'. For some the whole film industry, like most other aspects of our culture, is in the hands of the evil one. Our desire for holiness precludes us from partaking of the beast. We miss a great deal. Stories told in the media of film can have a profound effect upon us.

In 1994 and 1996 two films stood out clearly at the Oscar Award Ceremonies in Hollywood: *Schindler's List*, directed by Steven Spielberg, in 1994 and *Braveheart*, directed by Mel Gibson, in 1996. Both films received the award for Best Film. In a short film in which Mel Gibson was asked why he made the award-winning film he commented, 'I hope that they can't talk at the end of it. I hope they are so moved and so inspired by it that they have watched this great story and find something inside themselves.'

It had precisely that effect on Andy and our middle son Ben when they made a pilgrimage to Hoyts Ten Screen Cinema at the Pyramid Mall in Ithaca. Although it is in some regards a

Boys' Own fantasy, the passion of Sir William Wallace as he fought for Scottish freedom stirred the heart. The final scene, clearly reminiscent of the crucifixion, ending with Wallace's strong cry of 'freedom' as he lies on the rack of torture is among the most moving Hollywood has produced. It has provided hours of discussion about the passions of human life, of the depths to which humanity can sink and of the desperation in the human spirit for freedom.[28]

Schindler's List was no less powerful. A story is woven (in this case closer to historical truth than Gibson's film) which pierces the consciousness and leaves the mind numb at the horrific possibilities of human depravity. When Andy saw the picture on its release in England he wandered numbly through the Gateshead Metro Centre for an hour after the film finished. The effect on the soul was deeper than most church services ever attended. The journey home was accompanied with deep prayer both for Jewish sufferers of the Holocaust and for the murderers who perpetuated their suffering. Spielberg's film in its powerful emotional penetration does more to explain the Christian doctrine of depravity than a dozen well-argued sermons. What we perhaps know 'in our head' may be imparted through prophetic story-telling.

Both films have produced a change which is hard to deny. It is perhaps a redeeming feature of our culture that films portraying the remembrance of deep suffering and of great passion, and dealing with the themes of human depravity and freedom are honoured as the best of the season. Hollywood is not all bad!

Some may want to argue, 'Surely, neither Gibson nor Spielberg set out to produce a film inspired by the Holy Spirit.' We do not have information at hand to begin to answer that query. But it misses the point. The point is not so much the producer's intention but the way in which the Spirit of God can use such films to reveal more of God and his ways to us.

During its first week at our local cinema we went, as a family, to see the 1996 film, *Twister*. We had eagerly awaited its release as over the proceeding few months God had spoken to us many times through the imagery of whirlwinds. Therefore our attitude was one of expectation as we looked for God to speak to us during the film. We were not disappointed; the theme throughout the whole show spoke to us of commitment. A small group of people had a consuming passion: to chase tornadoes wherever they were found. One memorable line for us was when the characters were discussing the forces of 'twisters', measured by numbers from one to five. Someone asked if anyone had experienced an F5. The answer came from another that only one person had experienced an F5 and when asked what it was like had replied, 'An F5 is the finger of God.' We were greatly affected by the film and have even prayed, 'Lord, send a spiritual F5 to this city.'

In our book *Something Extraordinary is Happening*, we tell the story of Brian who found God speaking prophetically to him during the film *Forrest Gump*.[29] In the simple line 'There comes a time when there are no more stones left to throw' the Holy Spirit addressed Brian. The line comes in a poignant part of the story when a young woman comes face to face with some of the painful memories of her past. In the movie the line actually breaks the tension of the drama and most people end up laughing or at least smiling at that point. For Brian it had the opposite effect. Tears flowed fully and freely as God used *Forrest Gump* to speak truth to his heart. The story was used by the Spirit of God to bring deep release followed by repentance.

We received a letter from our good friends Darren and Jackie, sharing with us how God had spoken to a lady in their fellowship. He had spoken, prophetically, through the 1995 Disney film, *The Lion King.* They quoted her words:

> Simba has run away from his responsibilities and would not accept that he was the King. His late father Mufasa appears to him and chides him with these words: Simba you are more than what you have become.
>
> The Lord has shown me and indeed the church, that I am and the church can become more than what we have become.

Whatever the film-maker's intentions in these instances there are points at which God steps in. Now we are not saying that all films are prophetic or that the same movies will have the same effect on all people. What we are saying is that if we have eyes to see, our Father will communicate with us in far more varied and rich ways than we have allowed in the past. He is in the whole of life and his prophetic revelation comes in many ways.

Recovering prophetic story-telling in the church

We might then expect there to be a recovering of prophetic story telling in a new move of the Spirit of God. The creative imagination of the people of God is being fired again by the Holy Spirit! We are learning, like our Celtic forebears, to tell stories again.

Ray, one of a team of pastors in a nearby local church, is an artist who uses his art as a means of prophecy. Ray was a participant in a day of training we were hosting on prophecy. He suggested that he use a 'prophetic slide show' to demonstrate the powerful prophetic use of words and images together. We had never heard of such a thing but trusted Ray sufficiently to encourage him.

The 'slide show' consisted of a number of images, which Ray had painted and transferred to slides, juxtaposed against a lyrical narrative of a downcast warrior whose strength is renewed to fight another day. Much of the impact is lost without the pictures, but we include it as an instance of the creative use of imagination.

Awake O Knight

Is there no war, is there no pilgrimage? Is there none to carry Zion's banner? Who knows the way to Zion's hill overgrown with dense forest? Oh for the glimpse of this city of gold! Zeal's fire burnt to a smoking ember. How long will you be tied to the spell of sleep with chains of comfort for your bed chamber? Warrior, old from trying, when will your past seize its echoed speaking? The borrowed bread has lost its virtue and no longer enables you to fight. Darkness breathes its heavy threats. His shadowed lie creeps like a fog seeking to find its place in you while you languish in desert dreams. Your Captain prays to see you rise, hoping to stir you to your feet, hoping you will take your place.

Night threatens his chords of death and plays a dirge in tonal grey weaving spells in hypnotic song. The dawning bird cries, 'Oh Knight, why do you sleep the sleep of death? Man of war, who has robbed you of your sight? Who has cast your heart in stone, stolen your heart of fire? You lay in forest ablaze with colours that you do not perceive. Thinking you can stray from your Captain's eye, away from comrade and friend—your foe boldly sweeps seeking with lying tongue to capture and poison your memory; to crush your hope; to waste your passion in sweet deception. In your repose you lay internally wounded. If only you had eyes to see what spirits are upon you!

What powers of dark domain assail you! They rant and rage in terror, ready to condemn and accuse you day and night. They attempt to tear every promise from your heart. The battleground is strewn with the pieces of covenantal love now vanished from sight. You, whose Captain commissioned you to watch, pray, and build. While you sleep this sad gap has left you wanting. Truth mixed with treachery disguised in the customs of the day has cracked your wall, has opened you to dishonour your Captain's' name. Your thoughts escape the present battle, while dream prisoners wait for their release, knowing you hold the key. They wait in hope.

On, warrior of the day, face your darkness, repent and rise from the dead! Look into the Father's love—see the distance between you and his justice bridged in his cross. Draw near to this Holy Fire, 'Oh God, burn the dross of my selfish fear. Consume that which corrupts my imagination. Mend this divided man that I have become. Forgive my wilful blindness. I long to see who you are and who I am to be. Focus my upward call. Oh God, show me your way! I have shut my ear to your trumpet call and I have chosen sleep over war, but now I pray that in you I may rise and again fight the good fight of faith.

I wait for your strength, Oh my God. I wait for your word!

I will go before you. I will enable you to defend and occupy the land which is yours. You will volunteer freely in this day of battle. You are the warrior who stands in the day of battle. Standing with single-eyed resolve, your steady aim is without fear as you glare into the face of inferior foe. Victory is in the air. You stand armoured to win, muscles taut, practised and prepared for such a day as this. Strike your bow. Take back stolen land. This is the winning day. A day to praise the Captain of this victory band. For I am the strength of David's line. My Spirit will come upon you. You will bring down strongholds in my name. Look into the eye of the storm and know that the Captain of the Lord's hosts stands and fights for you.

Join your brothers and comrades. If you stand together you will cause many to be put to flight. Together you will be more than conquerors, you will be a redemptive force given to the land. Use the weapons of faith and prayer. Skilfully fight in covenantal love. Build your families. Rise to your destined victory. For my promise is with you.

Knight of the King of kings, rule and reign in his resurrected and ascended life. Put on the whole armour of God. Rise and fight and bring to the earth his peace.[30]

The impact of the words is reinforced by images of the warrior and his surroundings and by apt music which complements the whole.

We were all deeply moved. We identified with the warrior. We felt his pain was our pain. We wanted him to rise. We longed for his refreshment. When it came we felt ourselves refreshed. The prophetic slide show lasted only fifteen minutes but the intensity and profundity of story and picture penetrated the hearts of all who participated. God was present.

CHAPTER 7

PROPHETIC SIGNS IN
JOHN'S GOSPEL

Why does God use signs?

There is a story of St Colman, the cock, the mouse and the fly.[31] God wished to teach Colman diligence in his devotions, and Colman learned through the threefold sign of these simple gifts of God: the cock, the mouse and the fly. Perhaps the element of Celtic spirituality we find the hardest to come to terms with is its great austerity and treating the physical body with considerable harshness. The luxury of our chairs and beds bid us remain in middle-class comfort. Not so the pioneers of Christianity in Britain. Not just prayer, but prayer through the watches of the night in some personal discomfort was their daily fare.

The cock was provided by God to wake Colman at lauds, the first service of the daily office. Colman perceived that as a sign of God's kindness to him in not allowing him to sleep in! The signs of the mouse and the fly were more remarkable. The mouse would not allow Colman to sleep through the night watches. At the prescribed times the mouse would gently gnaw at his clothes or nibble at his ear. The fly would trot up and down the page of the psalm he was reading. If the man of God was called away for any reason, the fly would mark the exact line Colman had last read. When, in time, the three little friends died, Colman wrote in some remorse to Columba. He had perceived in them signs of God's grace to him. God cared, even in the smallest things.

We are beginning to learn that God communicates through the use of signs: concrete situations and events which speak profoundly of his purposes. We have been used to thinking of God in words and ideas for so long that to receive him in other ways seems a novelty! However, we need to remember that even the New Testament was written in a largely pre-literary era. Most people were, quite simply, illiterate. Truth was communicated to most people through the medium of story in which much was made of the symbolic and metaphorical use of circumstances and objects. We still recognise this in the popular phrase 'a picture is worth more than a thousand words'. The sweep of a sign can be grasped more quickly than a lengthy explanation. There are other elements of human personality to be engaged besides the cerebral: many of us are visual-concrete thinkers rather than conceptual-abstract.

Andrew Walker makes the point in his book *Telling the Story*, that the Reformation in Europe established the hierarchy of 'ear over eye'.[32] The material world was undervalued and the sensuous faculties of human personality were downgraded as reason (and its literary child) took pre-eminence.

Somewhere in the last few hundred years, most people in the Western churches lost something very precious: that God communicates through signs which point to God rather than words which try to explain him.

Prophetic sign in John's Gospel

Let's take a look at the example Jesus sets us in leading a prophetic lifestyle. In the record of the events of Jesus' life, revelation and truth from God are often shown to us prophetically. Through actions and pictures taken from everyday life and circumstances, Jesus declares great and important aspects of God's ways to us. Of the four Gospels John, helps us see this in the clearest way and speaks throughout of prophetic signs which Jesus explains in clear teaching *after* the sign has been revealed. It's quite significant to note that the revelation of the Father that Jesus brings comes first, not in plain words, but in prophetic symbol and action. Only after this initial prophetic enactment does Jesus teach plainly. In fact, the entire first half of John's Gospel is designed by the evangelist to demonstrate this very point. He tells us as much in chapter 20 as he summarises the Gospel. Eugene Peterson expresses it well in his interpretation 'Jesus provided far more God-revealing signs than are written down in this book. These are written down so you will believe that Jesus is the Messiah, the Son of God, and in the act of believing, have real and eternal life in the way he personally revealed it' (John 20:30–31 in *The Message*).

It's some of these 'God-revealing signs' which we want to look at in this chapter.

Wine from water

The first prophetic sign was the changing of water into wine at the wedding in Cana. This particular sign is a miraculous changing of one substance into another. John comments in this way: 'This act in Cana of Galilee was the first sign Jesus gave, the first glimpse of his glory' (John 2:11, The Message) showing us his insight into the prophetic nature of the action in its revelation of God.

This first sign is strange in a number of ways. It was evidently an extravagant action on Jesus' part. The sheer amount of wine he created would swamp the grandest of weddings. Estimates are in the region of 120 gallons—or over 700 bottles of the finest wine! Clearly, it was not merely a miracle to provide a frantic wedding host with more bubbly for the celebrations. Because of the nature of the sign something more is being said.

It's also interesting that this first of the sign-miracles is the changing of one substance into another. For many centuries alchemists tried unsuccessfully to do a similar thing. Their life's quest was to change one substance into another and the most publicised were their attempts to transmute base metals into gold or silver. It's the stuff dreams are made of. To turn something base and ordinary into something scarce and precious would result in untold riches.

Alchemy was actually the precursor of modern chemistry and first appeared around 100 AD in Alexandria, Egypt. It was a fusion of Greek and Oriental culture. Later the science attracted such medieval scholars as Roger Bacon (c 1220–1292, the Franciscan Friar and philosopher) and Albertus Magnus (c 1200–1280, the Dominican and Aristotelian scholar who taught Thomas Aquinas) and was admired by many princes including sixteenth-century Emperors Maximilian II (1527–1576) and his son Rudolf II (1552–1612). Alchemy was based on three key precepts. The first came from Aristotle's teachings that the basis for all material objects could be found in the four elements, fire, water, air and earth. The second precept was that all substances could be converted into one another. The third idea, taken from astrology, was that substances could be born, nourished and caused to grow through imperfect stages into a final perfect form. Alchemy was finally superseded by the advent of modern chemistry at the end of the eighteenth century. It has now long been realised that the quest of the alchemists was a futile one.

Yet Jesus had done the very thing the alchemists spent their lives trying to do and which modern chemistry tells us is impossible. He had requested six stone waterpots, each holding twenty or thirty gallons, to be filled with water and yet when the host tasted the water it had become wine. Jesus showed all who were present at the wedding that it was supernaturally possible for one substance to be changed into another. And thankfully, John recorded it so that for all generations it has stood as a prophetic sign showing that the intrinsic nature of one thing can be changed—with God all things are possible.

The plain teaching corresponding to the sign comes in the next chapter. It tells us that some time after this sign, Jesus went to Jerusalem and was visited one night by Nicodemus who was a Pharisee and a prominent leader among the Jews. Nicodemus said to him, 'Rabbi, we know you're a teacher straight from God. No one could do all the God-pointing, God-revealing acts you do if God weren't in on it' (John 3:2, *The Message*). Again, Peterson catches the essence of the meaning of the Gospel in speaking of the miracles as 'God pointing, God-revealing acts'.

There follows a discourse in which Jesus tells Nicodemus that he needs to be born again. It was clear to Nicodemus that Jesus was speaking of a change in nature. The new birth, birth from above of which he speaks seems a natural impossibility—not unlike the changing of one substance into another. Nicodemus questions this and receives the reply that it is only possible by the Spirit. Jesus had already shown through prophetic sign that supernaturally it was possible to change one thing into another. He had given them the prophetic sign of water into wine.

John chapters 2 and 3 need to be taken together, revealing through sign and teaching the great truth which works in the lives of all true believers: 'So if anyone is in Christ, there is a new creation: everything old has passed away: see, everything has become new' (2 Corinthians 5:17). The teaching illustrates one of the central truths of vital Christianity—people can have new life through Jesus. Those who have encounters with Jesus Christ find that their very natures can be changed. But of significance for us at present is that this great truth was first demonstrated in prophetic sign.

A well of water and eternal life

Chapter 2 also demonstrates the prophetic nature of sign and symbol as revelation from God. In the familiar story of the woman at the well Jesus illustrates a number of truths. He broke through all the customs of the day when he talked to the Samaritan woman. First, she was a woman and in that culture Jesus, as a single man, should not have approached the woman and spoken to her. To compound that difficulty, later in the story we find that she was also a woman of poor moral reputation. Secondly, she came from Samaria, and the Jews did not associate with the Samaritans. Simply by his actions Jesus was displaying a prophetic sign that the walls which had divided humanity were to come down. Paul's great truth that in Christ there is neither Jew nor Greek, male nor female is enacted by Jesus in his encounter with the Samaritan woman.

This woman had tried to satisfy her inner longings through sexual promiscuity. Five husbands had not helped and we are not given the impression that the man she lived with was any more effective. Her action in seeking to draw water to quench her thirst became prophetic of a deeper thirst—a spiritual thirst—which only Jesus could satisfy. He skilfully uses her present occupation (drawing water) to speak revelation from God about living water which springs from the heart. The need to draw water became a prophetic revelation of the inner heart condition of all people.

In this incident, and in those which follow, there is the interplay of prophetic symbolism declaring revelation through life and circumstance and the more open teaching which Jesus gives. In fact, the teaching becomes more often than not an interpretation of the prophetic sign.

Bread for the stomach and living bread

A not dissimilar occurrence is found in John chapter 6. Again, the sign relates to a crowd of people who find themselves with a particular need—in this case food. The crowds had followed Jesus, waiting on his every word and action to discover something of God for themselves. They were so keen that they didn't want to leave for a single hour: they might miss some great miracle or some inspiring words. Eating became a predicament. They needed food but couldn't bear to leave Jesus. It presented a problem which caused the disciples some consternation. It occasioned one of the great miracles of the Scriptures and the only one to be found in all four Gospels. We remember the miracle as the feeding of the 5,000, though in reality there were probably twice or three times that number present. It was customary only to count the men. Women and children were excluded from the figure. Nevertheless, a large crowd of folk were fed with food to spare.

This great sign provides Jesus with an opportunity to tell the crowd that he is living bread. The bread they had eaten merely met their bodily appetite–and only for a short while. The simple and everyday action of eating bread becomes a powerful prophetic tool pointing to God's revelation. People are more than their physical stomachs! There are inner needs, created by God, which need to be satisfied. There is a living bread which came down from heaven which is just as necessary, indeed, even more so. This bread is none other than the Lord himself. Again, prophetic sign and clear teaching go together.

Writing on the ground

There has been scholarly debate as to whether John 7:53–8:11 is an authentic part of the Gospel. There is sufficient weight that most Bible translations include the passage (though some have it in parenthesis). It is also one of the most memorable scenes in the Gospels which teaches that with God there is always forgiveness for sins.

There is apparent hypocrisy in the story. A woman caught in adultery is brought before Jesus, but not the man with whom she had sinned. Religious legalism rears its ugly head and 'justice' is demanded according to the law of Moses. What would Jesus do? With consummate wisdom Jesus suggests that the one among them who is without sin should cast the first stone. It did the trick! As they all admitted their own sinfulness, from the oldest down, none were willing to begin the cruel punishment of the poor woman. With God, when there is repentance, there is always forgiveness, always a second chance, always the slate is wiped clean.

But of interest to us are the two times Jesus wrote with his finger on the ground. We are not told what he wrote—it's not even hinted at. So it is not so much the content of the writing but the action of the writing that bears significance. In Exodus we are told: 'When God finished speaking with Moses on Mount Sinai, he gave him the two tablets of the covenant, tablets of stone, written with the finger of God' (Exodus 31:18).

The law was not only given by God in words but written on tablets with his finger. The religious leaders, in wanting to trap Jesus, present the cold harshness of the law—the very law written with the finger of God. And in response Jesus writes with his finger on the ground. The symbolism is powerful. It was not that he had come to destroy the law and prophets but to fulfil them. And in writing on the ground with his finger, Jesus is enacting a revelatory sign which shows he is completing the law. Mercy triumphs over judgement! And the religious leaders knew it. They had no answer and simply walked away.

Born blind and spiritual blindness

Chapter 9 of John reveals the same pattern. First, there is the prophetic sign of the man born blind whom Jesus heals. The physical sign then provides the platform for Jesus to teach about spiritual blindness. In the interchange with the Pharisees Jesus moves, as he does on many occasions, from discussion about something outward and temporal to something inner and eternal. There is at first debate about the man's physical blindness and the possibility of a real miracle taking place. In the interchange the religious leaders are loathe to believe that the man was ever blind in the first place. They were without faith and there was a huge issue, in the eyes of the Pharisees, about the authority of Jesus to perform miracles. However, towards the end of their discussion, Jesus turns the subject around to focus on spiritual blindness, telling the crowd that 'For judgment I have come into the world, so that the blind will see and those who see will become blind' (John 9:39).

The issue is turned from the possibility of miracles and the authority to perform them (two questions which are somewhat outward and directed away from the hearers) to the inner needs of all present. Religion often concerns others and their correctness and outward conformity to a tradition. Jesus turns the discussion round to the inner needs everyone has, in this case for spiritual sight.

Again it becomes clear that the physical blindness and healing of the man is a prophetic sign pointing to the revelation that all are blind until their eyes are opened by God. Certainly, the religious leaders feel the impact of the sign as they ask Jesus if he is referring to their blindness, as of course he is.

Died and lived again

The dead are not often raised! There have been notable cases. When Andy was a student at the Northern Baptist College, preparing for ministry, college staff and students alike were amazed at the story told by a local Anglican vicar of the raising to life of a Church Army captain who had died. Even in the life and ministry of Jesus those raised from the dead were few and far between. Lazarus had died. His sisters were in that initial period of shock, sorrow and grief which follow closely on the death of a loved one. But they were women of faith—faith in Jesus.

Yet Jesus didn't come. They had sent messages when

Lazarus was merely sick. If the Saviour had come then their brother would surely not have died. And now he had. There was something approaching accusation in Martha's voice as she complained to Jesus, 'If you had been here then Lazarus would not have died!'

Jesus was no hard-hearted miracle worker. Even knowing that his Father would answer his prayers for Lazarus lying in the grave, seeing the tears and sorrow of the sisters Jesus himself wept. Deeply moved he calls the dead Lazarus to come out of the tomb. In a wondrous miracle life is breathed into the corpse of a dead man, his spirit returns and two sisters are more grateful to God at that moment than any other people on the earth.

But the raising to life is a powerful sign which points beyond itself to the short time to come when Jesus himself would die and be raised, not merely to a few more years of mortality but to life everlasting and incorruptible. It is interesting that, in the way John tells the story of Jesus, it was after the raising of Lazarus that the plot was set in motion which would lead to the crucifixion of Jesus (John 11:45).

This sign of all signs seems to point beyond this life to a better resurrection which will not be followed by death. It is rare for that very reason—we await the fullness of time when death will be swallowed up finally by life. Just as all physical and emotional healing point like signposts to a time when there will be no more sickness, the raising to life of one who has died shouts to us that death is not the end.

With hindsight, following the resurrection the disciples would look back and say to one another, 'We should have known! Didn't he give us the prophetic sign by raising Lazarus from the grave? Through that alone we should have realised that death would not be able to hold him.'

Foot washing and servanthood

In warm countries people tend to wear sandals. It gets too hot for shoes and socks. It's nice to feel the warmth directly on your toes, to let the air circulate. But it has drawbacks. Feet get dirty and begin to smell. For the sake of good conversation and to maintain friendship it's best to wash feet regularly, particularly when you're going to be in close proximity with folk at dinner!

For those reasons it was a custom in Jesus' day for the servants of the house or the women to wash the feet of guests. It was not a particularly pleasant job nor one which household heads would take on. When Jesus took the task upon himself it caused not a little embarrassment among his followers. It just wasn't right. There was an uneasy feeling for many present as Jesus took the menial task and found himself cleaning the sweat and dirt from the feet of those who looked up to him. Peter, as was his common response, took the lead. He was a little indignant, even refusing to let Jesus near his feet, giving in only after a stern rebuke by his friend and master.

The prophetic symbolism was potent. The new faith was not to be about position and hierarchy. It was to be a way characterised by service to one another, by each taking the lower place, the menial and the despised. Discipleship with Jesus was not to be a matter of word but deed following the example of one who had voluntarily become the least.

There are other prophetic signs in John's Gospel. We have chosen these few to whet the appetite for discovering the voice of God in sign, wonder, prophetic action and the everyday circumstances of life.

CHAPTER 8

EARTHQUAKE, WIND AND FIRE

Let the heavens be glad, and let the earth rejoice;
let the sea roar, and all that fills it;
let the field exult, and everything in it.
Then shall all the trees of the forest sing for joy
before the Lord; for he is coming

Psalm 96:11–13a

Pensacola is located in the panhandle of north-west Florida and offers fun in the sun, beautiful beaches, wonderful parks, great attractions and plenty of museums and history to explore. Pensacola Beach is a year-round vacation place and is recognised as 'the world's whitest beach', having sand that looks, they say, white as sugar.

At the beginning of October 1995 we listened in amazement as the second hurricane hit the Florida panhandle in less than two months. In Hurricane Opal torrential rain and winds up to 170 miles per hour lashed the Gulf of Mexico. According to the National Public Radio morning news, Hurricane Aaron, eight weeks earlier, was the first hurricane to hit this part of

Florida since 1926. Two in the space of nine weeks was quite astonishing. What was equally amazing was that the coming of the great wind coincided with the beginning of a great move of God focussed on an Assembly of God church in Brownsville Pensacola where in the first six weeks of meeting 80,000 people passed through revival meetings. By the end of the year around 12,000 people had made a commitment to Christ in the nightly meetings. And that was just the beginning. At the time of writing the revival continues in its intensity. The natural weather conditions matched and spoke dramatically and prophetically of a great wind of the Spirit which mightily touched that part of the world. Could it be that God still speaks to us through the natural signs and wonders of the creation—if only we have ears to hear and eyes to see?

Celts and creation

All praise be yours, my Lord, through Brothers Wind and Air,
And fair and stormy, all the weather's moods,
By which you cherish all that you have made.

St Francis of Assisi

The process of industrialisation and, more recently, the revolution in information technology have added immensely to our lives. We can hardly imagine what life was like before centrally heated homes, cars that run virtually trouble free, washing machines, shopping centres and the Information Superhighway. Indeed, we have often pondered how people used to write books in days gone by (all of twenty years) without the immense benefits of fast computers and the Internet to do speedy, reliable and accurate research. Though the new technology is frightening to many folk, we are convinced it is a wonderful creative tool which God has given us. Of course, our children are far more adept with the new technology than we are! To them it's quite natural.

But, if truth be told, we have also lost something, which God is graciously restoring little by little. Like a jigsaw puzzle being pieced together we are beginning to discern a pattern we have not seen for a long time. Somewhere along the way we lost touch with creation—the 'naturalness' of it, the unprocessed quality, the sheer beauty of it as it came from the creator's hands. To the Hebrew mind there was no incongruity with the seas, fish, fields, grass, trees and stones giving praise to God—almost as if the whole of creation is animated with the sense and presence of the creator. The whole reveals him and shouts his praise.

What has been uncovered is a different view of creation. Different in that humanity is perceived as being much more in touch and at one with creation. Different, too, in that God reveals himself more fully in creation than we modern Christians have allowed. Celtic Christians had a similarly holistic view of creation. The stones and the trees, the wind and the waves become friends and messengers from God as God reveals himself through creation.

The famous Celtic Christian prayer 'Patrick's Breastplate' helps us see their understanding.[33] In the prayer Patrick says:

> I bind unto myself today
> the virtues of the starlit heaven,
> the glorious sun's life-giving ray,
> the whiteness of the moon at even,
> the flashing of the lightning free,
> the whirling wind's tempestuous shocks,
> the stable earth, the deep salt sea,
> around the eternal rocks.

What was Patrick alluding to? In another version of the hymn, Patrick, in danger of his life, prays:

> At Tara in this fateful hour,
> I place all heaven with its power,
> and the sun with its brightness,
> and the snow with its whiteness,
> and fire with all the strength it hath,
> and lightning with its rapid wrath,
> and the winds with their swiftness along the path
> and the earth with its starkness: all these I place,
> by God's almighty help and grace,
> between myself and the powers of darkness.

Was this a kind of animism—all natural elements infused with a spiritual power as in paganism? Some have argued that the Christian Celtic tradition was an admixture of both Christian and pagan beliefs. Indeed, some Christian Celtic spirituality has an unfamiliar ring to it. However, simply because something is outside of our present frame of reference does not make it untrue. We want to encourage an openness to the unfamiliar and to find revelation of God outside our comfort zones. That is the way of growth.

Undoubtedly, with every expression of Christianity there is a 'clothing' of the faith in cultural forms which are meaningful to the present generation. Just take a look at the many current Christian books which borrow extensively from post-Freudian psychological perspectives and from management practice. Not all of it fits within a biblical framework. But then much of it does. The truth of God revealed in Scripture is echoed in much of creation and human understanding. All truth is God's truth. Different movements within society often push Christians to re-examine their own roots in the biblical tradition. In the nineteenth century a humanistic objection to slavery caused Christians to look again at the Scriptures and to find that humanistic reasoning about the value of every human being reflected the truth of God in the Bible. In this century the secular women's movement raised a voice against the injustices perpetrated by men on women and made us look again at the Scriptures. Many of us have discovered that women and men are truly equal and that there is a need for radical rethinking of church structures. We have also realised that what many environmentalists have been saying is true according to the word of God. There is a stewardship of creation which the church has been ignorant of for some time.

What then of the Celts? In a culture very close to nature the Celts lived a Christianity which saw God intimately involved in the whole of life. The stones, wind and waves are not animated with inferior 'spirits', but the whole of creation is animated with the Spirit of God who upholds all things by the word of his power. If only we would open our eyes to see there is much revelation from God in the things around us.

Where is the voice of God?

As our senses became heightened to an awareness that God could and would speak to us through nature and the everyday circumstances of our lives, we started to look for his voice. And the more we looked, the more we became aware of God's speaking. A frequent question on our lips is, 'God, are you speaking to us in this?'

We were on our way to a preaching engagement, driving to a church with our hosts. As the car came to a halt, we heard a loud miaowing sound through the open window. A cat jumped onto the bonnet purring and rubbing itself against the front window. Then it moved around to the open side window, and started to rub itself against the driver, sounding like a little lion. We all watched in amazement, as none of us had seen a cat behave in such a way before. Strangely, we had been speaking to our hosts moments before about prophetic lifestyle. It was almost in jest that we prayed, 'God is this you? Please reveal to us what you are speaking.'

A little later during the meeting, as we worshipped, a scene came to mind from C.S. Lewis's *The Horse and His Boy*[34] Shasta, the main character in the book, finds himself in the Tombs of the Ancient Kings. He has to spend the night alone and the silent stones begin to frighten him. The boy feels something touching him and discovers that the movement comes from a cat. Shasta is relieved at the sight and touch of the large and solemn cat. The cat leads him from the tombs and guards him during the night, giving the boy comfort during a fearful time. Later in the book it is revealed that it was Aslan who had appeared to him in the form of a cat to comfort Shasta among the houses of the dead. Through the remembrance of the story God spoke clearly to Jane, 'Comfort and calm fears,' and gave us the direction for the meeting. The direction was confirmed as during the meeting God came in great power, though in one of the gentlest ways we have seen. Writing to us later people said how gentle God had been and how he had calmed the fears of those who were a little fearful of the move of God.

God has often used nature to mirror what he is doing in the spiritual realm. Early one spring, the whole area of the Tyne Valley in Northumberland flooded. It wasn't just a little flood: the River Tyne burst its banks. Our children were sent home from school, as the roads were quickly becoming impassable. We stood on the higher road near our house and looked in amazement over the valley. No longer did we see the clearly defined landscape. A sea of water covered everything. Where had all the water come from? Even bridges over the river became dangerous as the water lapped over them and they shook under the power of the flood. Normally the water level is thirty feet below these centuries old structures. Later, as the waters started to abate, we were amazed to see how large oak trees had been tossed along the river as if they were little twigs. Again we heard God speaking prophetically. He was flooding the church, and nothing in the way of the Spirit could remain untouched. We also used the prophetic signs as a direction for prayers. 'Lord, as we've seen the natural floods, please continue a spiritual flood.' And, 'Lord, if there is anything in our lives preventing the flow of your Spirit, please uproot it.'

Just a few weeks later we were driving along the valley when we noticed how dry the river was, lower than normal. Again, we asked, 'God, what are you showing us in this?' As we asked we realised the spiritual truth that we can quickly 'dry up'; that it is necessary to always have the 'river of life' flowing in us. It isn't sufficient to have experienced the watering of the Holy Spirit once; it needs to be an ongoing thing in our lives.

Of course, God using nature as an illustration of what he is doing isn't new. One very clear example in Scripture is found in the Book of Jonah. Called by God to proclaim his word to the Ninevites, Jonah had become disobedient. Following the large fish incident Jonah is recommissioned and eventually preaches to the city of Nineveh. Astonishingly, he becomes angry when the people of that great city repent and turn to God. He had announced impending judgment, proclaiming that the city would be overthrown, but God showed mercy and spared them. God came to Jonah again and caused a large gourd to grow (a palm-like bush) to give Jonah shelter. When the bush withered Jonah again became angry and God spoke again. He used the gourd to prophetically expose Jonah's attitude of heart, and to allow Jonah to feel something of God's own heart for the people of Nineveh. Jonah's gourd was full of prophetic symbolism.

The lights have changed!

We experienced God speaking to us through nature on a personal level. We knew that God was calling us to leave the area where we had ministered for eleven years, but we were unsure where we were to go next or when we were to move on. One night, as a small group gathered to pray in our home, a clear word was given to several of us. We were considering Ezekiel 1:4 which speaks of a great whirlwind. The picture is very dramatic and the colour amber is mentioned. For some reason the word 'amber' struck a number of us as important. At that point we weren't sure of what this simple word might mean, but we prayed that God would show us. As we considered it our minds were drawn to reflect on the idea of traffic lights. Like all young would-be drivers it was drilled into us by our driving instructors that at road junctions amber meant wait and get ready. It indicates a state of waiting as something is about to change. Our prayers became, 'Lord, show us when it's green.'

Every day as we drove from our home in the Tyne Valley we admired the view over the often spectacular valley. Sometimes in that spring and early summer it was covered in mist which we gazed down upon with the exhilarating feeling of being above the clouds. But often it was just a carpet of amber and yellow as the oil-seed rape fields were in full bloom. As the weeks passed, the direction of our immediate future started to unfold and a decision needed to be made. One day as we drove out of our street, we looked over the valley, and almost overnight it had become green. The brilliant amber of the rape fields lasts a short time as the crop greens for the harvest. God spoke to us, the amber had turned to green. It signified a time to move, a time to go.

Of course, someone else has used the fields to speak prophetically! Jesus used the fields to illustrate the need for workers to gather people into the kingdom. In John chapter 4, as he saw the Samaritans coming to him, he turned to the disciples and said, 'Look around you, and see how the fields are ripe for harvesting.' In fact, Jesus used the prophetic sign of the harvest on two other recorded occasions. In Matthew chapter 9 he had great compassion on the crowd and then in Luke chapter 10 he sent out seventy disciples into various towns and villages. The message is quite clear. Look at nature and the Father will bring a revelation to you.

And parking spaces too!

Who hasn't from time to time prayed in desperation, 'Lord, I really need to find a parking space. I'm late!' Larry experienced something more. After twenty-five years of work in the technology field within the same university, Larry lost his job. Downsizing, cutbacks and reorganisation left him redundant for the first time in his life. A temporary consultancy post opened up, but at a drastically reduced salary. Larry remained optimistic, began the job search (all over the USA) and continued to drive to work each day. After some weeks Larry noticed that each day, whatever time he arrived at work, there would be just one parking space available. Anyone who has tried to park on a busy university campus will know that, in itself, that is a small miracle! Yet day after day, the little miracle kept happening. Larry shared the strange phenomenon with us. We prayed and Jane perceived it to be a prophetic sign that there would be a job open for Larry yet again. For seven months Larry continued the consultancy work, and for seven months every single day there was just one parking space left. Then out of the blue and to much rejoicing a new position opened at the same level and salary which Larry had left months previously. It was a sign of God's abundant goodness.

Bearing signs in our body

These days some of God's people are starting to carry revelation from God in their physical bodies. We became aware of this while ministering in Lancashire. We were in conversation with a leader of a church which had wholeheartedly embraced renewal. He told us of a lady in the congregation who had stood firmly against the renewal movement. Our friend patiently continued to visit her and share about all that God was doing. After eight months the lady cried out to God, asking that he would show her if the 'blessing' was genuine or not. God revealed himself so that she could no longer argue against the move of the Spirit. The revelation came when her hip joint was displaced from its socket. She was reminded that a similar thing happened to Jacob when he wrestled with God. As God brought understanding she realised that she too had struggled against God.

At the same time her neck became stiff—and everybody knows what the Bible says about stiff necks! But at the time the intense pain she felt in her neck was no laughing matter. She could hardly turn her head. But through it God spoke, telling her she was spiritually a stiff-necked person. When she began to realise God was speaking through these prophetic signs in her body, her attitude changed. Thankfully, she was able to receive God's word to her, received healing and, subsequently, dealt with the issue God was speaking about. The prophetic sign in her body was an action of God's mercy. Her testimony now is that she is more aware of God's grace and has a greater liberty in the spirit than ever before.

Jane herself has experienced similar physical manifestations. We were hosting a day seminar on 'Women and Men . . . Heirs together of the Father's Grace'. The seminar is among a series of equipping days in which we look at a subject of practical value in some depth, using a variety of approaches to teaching and learning. On this particular day we wanted to explore the whole area of women and men working together and being released together in the anointing of God. After the seminar had concluded, the arch in Jane's foot seemed to collapse and for the next few days she was limping in pain. The Lord spoke to her and said that she was prophetically carrying in her body the pain of the church limping on one leg. For centuries women have had been excluded from many aspects of ministry. Men have done their best but much experience and gifting was neglected because it was believed that women should have no part in such things. The Body of Christ has been limping: the church has not functioned as intended. Three weeks later Jane was in Toronto for the 'Releasers of Life' women's conference. On the evening of the first day towards the end of the ministry time, Jane's arch collapsed again. During the conference the teaching was remarkably similar to the seminar we had hosted. God was speaking the same message and both times Jane carried the message physically and prophetically. For the rest of the conference Jane limped and was in pain. Again God spoke, more strongly and more clearly, that the church was in pain because it was limping on one leg.

A couple of months later, Jane again received prophetic

revelation through physical symptoms. This time she was covered with spots! Many people offered various suggestions as to the cause of the rash, but nothing seemed to fit. After a few days God spoke clearly to Jane—there's a poison in the body! The word given served as a forewarning to us. We had no knowledge of anything to be concerned about at that time. However, we shared and prayed with others in leadership. We discerned that there was indeed 'a poison in the body'. Several months later, after continual prayer and much wisdom, the situation was resolved.

Since then carrying a prophetic word in this way has happened several more times. One other is worthy of note. This was different from the previous occasions mentioned in that in this instance discernment came through another person.

Jane had backache, not something she was prone to. It was a niggly, annoying, constant pain. Also, we were in the middle of hosting a conference—a very inconvenient time to have backache! During one of the ministry team prayer times Jane requested prayer for healing. One of the women on the team, who has strong prophetic anointing, came forward and declared that the pain was a prophetic sign. The Lord was saying that the backbone of the church was weak. The church needed to be supported on the proper foundation of the apostles and prophets. In the following meeting there was a great prophetic release. The backache left with the declaration of the prophetic word.

CHAPTER 9

SWIMMING AGAINST THE FLOW

The heretical imperative

In 1969 sociologist Peter Berger published his landmark book *A Rumour of Angels*.[35] For the best part of a hundred years scholars in most disciplines had considered religion of any kind to be *passé*, an irrelevance to the knowledge and maturity of the human race. Religion, faith and all God-talk belonged to a bygone, more primitive and superstitious age. In theology the logical progression resulted in the mid-1960s statement that 'God is dead'.

But things began to change. The demise of religion was somewhat exaggerated! In the Christian church at the very moment that her theologians were announcing God's death, the Spirit of God was beginning a new stirring which dramatically changed the face of the church.

Some academics, including Berger himself, began to take a fresh look at religion in society and in many ways sociologists began to take the lead. Berger followed his *Rumour* with *The Heretical Imperative*.[36] His thesis was that in every generation there is a heretical imperative—a choice which takes the individual outside of the status quo and establishment trends. In ages when religion was predominant the heretical imperative took people away from the establishment mentality of the church/state edifice. In a society which has relegated religion from the premier league, the heretical imperative is to choose again the way of religious life in the face of growing secularism. Berger made a powerful argument. To find faith in a secular society is to take the heretical imperative.

We want to borrow his phrase for in many respects to seek to live a prophetic lifestyle will mean making such a choice. When most of religion is outward and related to form and organisation, to take the inner way, to discover the voice of God, to find his communication in everything around us may well be considered the heretical way. It is not the way of establishment. It is swimming against the flow.

Equally, to live prophetically will mean swimming against the flow of the 'anything-goes' culture of postmodernism. The liberty of the Spirit is not the same as the licence of 'if it feels good do it'. Listening attentively to the voice of God will always lead to holiness and a desire to live like Jesus. Also, we will want to swim against the flow of the radical individualism of postmodernity and find some sense of community, togetherness and connectedness. By the same token a Christian prophetic lifestyle will be rooted in Trinitarian orthodoxy. We are not seeking mystical experiences for the sake of being mystical! The truth is that to know the Christian God—Father, Son and Holy Spirit—means that we will be led into deep spiritual experiences. To live prophetically will be to swim against the flow of vague New Age mysticism.

Prophets against the flow

The prophets in the Old Testament were not strangers to the heretical imperative. Jeremiah, Hosea, Amos and their comrades found themselves called by God to swim against the flow both of their society and of the established direction of their religion. Religion had become an outward thing and no longer pleased God. Amos prophesied some of the harshest things in all the Bible when he said:

> I hate, I despise your festivals, and I take no delight in your solemn assemblies. Even though you offer me your burnt offerings and grain offerings, I will not accept them; and the offerings of well-being of your fatted animals I will not look upon. Take away from me the noise of your songs; I will not listen to the melody of your harps. But let justice roll down like waters, and righteousness like an everflowing stream.
>
> (Amos 5:21–24)

Hosea lived a remarkable prophetic sign. Incredulously, God told him to love a woman who already had a lover and was an adulteress (Hosea 3). The reason? That God wanted Hosea to live prophetically as a sign that the Lord himself loved Israel even though she had many 'lovers' and lived in spiritual adultery. In the strict Mosaic legal code the adulteress would be stoned (Deuteronomy 22). However, God himself urged Hosea to swim against the flow of legalism to demonstrate love and mercy.

The boy Samuel, who was to become a great prophetic figure, was born in a generation when the 'word of the Lord was rare . . . visions were not widespread' (1 Samuel 3:1) In his time, too, religion had become merely outward. Samuel was to live against the flow. He learned the lesson well when in later years he was commissioned to anoint a new king to replace

Saul. God told him then: 'Do not look on his appearance or on the height of his stature, because I have rejected him; for the LORD does not see as mortals see; they look on the outward appearance, but the LORD looks on the heart' (1 Samuel 16:7). Though Jesse's older sons were fine and handsome, tall and athletic, God was not interested in the outward appearance. His way has always been to do with the inner and not the outer.

The teaching of Jesus

The Sermon on the Mount in Matthew chapters 5–7 is perhaps the most radical statement of swimming against the flow ever written. Again and again Jesus assaults our sensibilities by saying that which we least expect. His opening gambit sends the mind reeling. It is the poor who are blessed, not the rich! It is those who mourn who are blessed not those who are happy! It's those who are hungry who are blessed and not the already filled! He continues by teaching that even an outward law-keeping is insufficient in the kingdom of God. The outward act of murder is begun in the inner thoughts of hatred, the outward act of adultery is already present in impure thoughts. And when someone abuses and wrongs you, you are to return blessing and not retaliation. Even enemies are to be loved and not hated. Piety, prayer and fasting are to be inner things and not for outward congratulation. The material issues of life which consume so much time and energy are to be overridden in a bid for simplicity of life in trust of a loving Father who knows all our needs.

The words of Jesus are against the flow today as they were against first-century culture. Through the long centuries of the church we have struggled with the extraordinarily radical teaching of Jesus. But it was not just teaching. The master lived the principles he professed. When accused he refused to answer back, even to acquit himself of false charges. When savagely and mercilessly beaten and crucified his words were words of love and forgiveness. Jesus raised up a different spirit which we are to take as our example in serving God.

Not forgetting Paul

Paul clearly received the direction of his life from Jesus. His clearest expressions of raising up a different spirit come in the letter to the Romans:

> Let love be genuine; hate what is evil, hold fast to what is good; love one another with mutual affection; outdo one another in showing honour. Do not lag in zeal, be ardent in spirit, serve the Lord. Rejoice in hope, be patient in suffering, persevere in prayer. Contribute to the needs of the saints; extend hospitality to strangers. Bless those who persecute you; bless and do not curse them. Rejoice with those who rejoice, weep with those who weep. Live in harmony with one another; do not be haughty, but associate with the lowly; do not claim to be wiser than you are. Do not repay anyone evil for evil, but take thought for what is noble in the sight of all. If it is possible, so far as it depends on you, live peaceably with all. Beloved, never avenge yourselves, but leave room for the wrath of God; for it is written, 'Vengeance is mine, I will repay, says the Lord.' No, 'if your enemies are hungry, feed them; if they are thirsty, give them something to drink; for by doing this you will heap burning coals on their heads.' Do not be overcome by evil, but overcome evil with good.
>
> (Romans 12:9–21)

This passage is sometimes misunderstood as a passage of judgment towards the end. 'Burning coals' is, in some way or other, to judge the enemy. In fact, coals would be carried in this way to light a new hearth. The inference is that enemies will be comforted, warmed and not judged when we feed them and give them something to drink. Enemy love is swimming against the flow. It's interesting that most of the commentaries on Paul dwell on the doctrinal parts of his letters. Huge volumes are written on the meaning of his teaching about redemption, justification and the eternal purpose of God. Little is written about his experiential, practical teaching. Perhaps it is because the challenge is so great. To live as he suggests would be to swim against the flow of our culture and even against the flow of most church culture. To take that way is, however, so important. It is the heretical imperative we must choose.

Raising up another spirit

Perhaps one of the major lessons we have learned in prophetic lifestyle is to 'raise up a different spirit'. The words of Jesus and Paul challenge us with amazing force. The kingdom of God is truly an 'upside-down kingdom'. The values and mores of the world are reversed in the kingdom of God.

One of the harder things ministers, missionaries (and probably all of us from time to time) face are the judgments of fellow believers. To our shame, criticism, judgement and condemnation often characterise the family of God rather than affirmation, love and forgiveness. We have agonised at times when we have heard that 'so and so' or 'such a church' are speaking against us or, in one instance, even praying against us. It hurts deeply. It cuts, too, when we discover some of the ugly rumours that are spread abroad about the way we choose to follow Christ. 'Church abuse', as it has come to be known in some circles, is prevalent. What do we do? We need to learn to raise up a different spirit. It is time for some of God's children to say 'enough is enough' and to begin to live differently, however we may be provoked.

Ian Bradley points out in his work on Columba that 'benediction' or blessing was a large part of Celtic Christian spirituality. He comments: 'The emphasis of the Columban Church on benediction was part of a much wider appreciation in Celtic Society of the power of the spoken word. Both blessings and cursing were regarded almost as physical actions which had the effect of transmitting good or evil.'[37]

In many parts of the church today we have begun to rediscover the truth of the power of words. In living prophetically we want to speak words of blessing, words which build up not pull down and destroy. It is salutary to watch any of the popular soap operas on TV to see how much of the dialogue is negative, back-biting and destructive. It is equally valuable to listen to conversation in the average church business meeting! It's time to raise up a different spirit.

We have had some fun in our family as we have sought to apply this principle. It's quite astonishing how much we actually say which is not edifying. Mary-Audrey Raycroft, one of the pastors of the Toronto Airport Christian Fellowship, teaches that prophetic words ought to 'build up, cheer up or lift up'. We adopted the phrase for our family and added, 'If you can't do those things then it's best to shut up!'

On one of those long and often boring drives family nerves can get a little frayed around the edges. It becomes easy to say cutting things which we don't really mean but which have the effect of winding everybody else up.

'I've an idea,' Andy said on one such trip. 'Why don't we put principles into practice? Only speak if you can build up, lift up or cheer up.'

We drove in silence for the next five minutes. One of the kids eventually piped up, 'Hey dad, this is *really* hard!'

It served as a valuable lesson to the whole family. It's time to begin living against the flow.

On one occasion St Brendan asked St Ita what most pleased and displeased God. Her reply was quite simple: 'Three things that please God most are true faith in God with a pure heart, a simple life with a grateful spirit, and generosity inspired by charity. The three things that most displease God are a mouth that hates people, a heart harbouring resentments, and confidence in wealth.'[38]

Interestingly, on the negative side she mentions first a hateful mouth. We *do* need to learn that. More positively, faithfulness, purity, simplicity, gratefulness, generosity and love are the things that most please God. To begin to live with those values on a day-to-day basis would be to raise up a different spirit.

Aidan's different spirit

Celtic Britain suffered under tribal bickering and territorial strife. In 617 the king of Northumbria was ousted from his throne. The king's son, Oswald, escaped to Iona and for the next seventeen years learned the way of Christ. In 634 he wrested the throne from the Welsh king Cadwollan and sought to establish Christianity within his kingdom. One of his first actions as king was to ask the Iona community to send a missionary to Northumbria to teach the way of Christ. The abbot at Iona responded by sending Corman who returned some time later after a journey of fruitlessness. Corman did not like the Northumbrians. He spoke to them at length about the wrath of God and their sinfulness and waywardness. He told them of God's anger, of the eternal pit 'where lost souls are leaping to and fro in silent agony, suffering for their sins, where bound with chains until the day of doom in torment the rebellious angels writhe . . .'[39]

He was not successful! On his return he called the Northumbrian people 'hard-hearted churls'. Upon hearing the report Aidan responded:

> The tender infant takes but milk at first, not meat and other stronger kinds of food. I pray thee, didst thou tell them of the love of Christ—his love divine—transcending all other loves—so wide and free that even the universe cannot contain it all, which caused the Son of God to feel for us in grief, to pray for those who did him wrong and give his life a ransom for mankind? The love of Christ—that wins and conquers all! I would not blame thee, brother, but methinks it was thy method, not thy theme that failed.[40]

The abbot was so pleased with Aidan's reply to Corman that he decided to send him instead! In the gentleness of the Spirit of Christ, Aidan began to win the people of Northumbria.

CHAPTER 10

PROPHETIC INTERCESSION

It sounded as though they were in great pain. Had we not experienced this a number of times before, maybe one of us would have asked if there was anything we could do. Instead, Jane made her way over to the three women, squatting and crouching on the floor together, and simply asked God to continue his work. 'Increase all that you are doing, Father. Give greater revelation. Let them feel as you feel. Let them know your heart.'

The groans, murmurs and occasional screams lasted for the best part of an hour. The three women were from three different churches and had begun to pray with one another. As the Holy Spirit rested on them they each began to weep and pray as God gave insight. The groaning and crying out had started as each in turn seemed as if they were, for all the world, about to give birth. Then, as their praying continued, prophetic words were released. It was as if each knew the inner thoughts of the others before they were spoken. We watched and prayed for them as they entered into what we have come to know as 'prophetic intercession'.

Not just a shopping list

Intercession, at its best, is an agreeing with the heart, mind and will of God. It is a spiritual perception of what is burning in our Father's heart and an agreeing in prayer with it. It is a revelation of the divine heart which has a profound effect spiritually, emotionally and, at times, physically on the intercessor. As such, it is more than just coming to God with a list of requests and more than praying for a specific person or issue. It seems that God actually reveals just a tiny part of his heart, and the revelation produces a physical reaction and a depth of interceding that we are only just beginning to experience. Of course, even in the most intense prophetic intercession it is only a small part of the Father's heart which is perceived. A full revelation of God's heart would crush the human spirit. While we recognise that we all need to intercede and pray, for some it is a deeper gifting. These are the ones we are learning to term 'prophetic intercessors'.

Marian describes what it feels like when she experiences the Spirit in this way:

> Suddenly I would begin to feel deeply some thing related to the prayer being prayed or the vision being shared. Sometimes I would weep, grieving more deeply than ever I would normally. This grief could not be contained and I would begin to shout or scream or moan while weeping uncontrollably. In each case it was almost as if God was revealing a small part of his heart to me, only what I could endure but pushing that endurance to the very limit till I felt I could contain no more.

Cathy has on many occasions felt the weight of intercession;

> It is a feeling of a broken heart. I pray for God's revelation of that feeling. I don't know what is on God's heart specifically until I open my mouth and then I am flooded with emotions. And to those emotions he adds words.

Of course, it is not really new. We only need to read the Book of Daniel to find a similar thing. Throughout the book God prophetically reveals his heart to Daniel through vision. Daniel's response is to be drawn into deeper intercession (chapter 9), with sackcloth and ashes. God responds with further prophetic revelation as the angel again comes to Daniel. There is a process of revelation and prayer which underlies Daniel's intercession. It was not prayer 'in the dark'.

Examples of this deep intercession permeate the Celtic church.

Such was Cuthbert's zeal for prayer that sometimes he would keep vigil for three or four straight nights without ever sleeping in his bed. Cuthbert was so filled with sorrow for sin, and so aflame with heavenly yearnings, that he could never finish mass without shedding tears. As was only fitting, he would initiate the holy ritual he was celebrating by offering himself to God with a contrite heart. His people were encouraged to lift their hearts and give thanks to the Lord God more by the yearnings of his own heart than by the sound of his voice, more by his sighs than his preaching. Often he would be the first to burst into tears, tears of compassion, as they were pouring out their sins.[41]

As with all forms of prophetic lifestyle, prophetic intercession is not a static thing, but a growing, developing part of our walk with God. For most of the intercessors it started as an individual experience but has developed to include a corporate aspect.

Marian shares how, for her, the intercession developed:

Last spring the whole area of intercession seemed to shift. Up to this point it was an individual thing for me. Quite suddenly it began to involve more than one person. At one meeting three or four people began to pray together. The Holy Spirit began to give words or pictures to one person and as the impressions were verbalised we all began to realise that the Spirit was speaking to each of us the same things at the same time. This was also accompanied by strong manifestations like weeping, shouting, laughing and pounding on the floor. This kind of intercession has happened several times in the last few months. It's as if the Lord has placed us together and has given each one a piece of a puzzle and the intercession is accomplished by everyone acting together and being willing to lay our individual pieces of the puzzle down to complete the picture.

More than words can tell

During another night I heard a voice—I do not know whether it was within me or beside me, God only knows—whose words I could not understand, except the final sentence: 'He who laid down his life for you, it is he that speaks within you.' And I awoke full of joy. And some time later I saw him praying within me: I was, as it were, inside my own body and I could hear his voice. He was praying most powerfully. I was dumbfounded, wondering who it could be praying within me; but at the end of the prayer he said that he was the Spirit. And I awoke, remembering the apostle's words: 'The Spirit helps us in our weakness; for we do not know how to pray as we ought, but the Spirit himself intercedes for us with sighs too deep for words.'[42]

St Patrick

From our observations and conversations with friends who are gifted in prophetic intercession, it seems that there is a growing process. Joan*,[43] another intercessor, shared with us that at first she wondered whether the physical manifestations were from God. At first she found herself bending as she prayed. The bending action would coincide with a deep sense of the presence of God and direction in prayer. If she resisted the physical sign, then her praying was less effective. She realised that the physical manifestation related in some way to her intercession. As she gradually yielded to God she found that she also began to groan as she prayed. Again, Joan was a little reluctant to enter in fully to the new form of praying. In time she came to receive it as a way of praying that is beyond words and which resembles in some ways what Paul speaks of in the letter of Romans.

> Likewise the Spirit helps us in our weakness; for we do not know how to pray as we ought, but that very Spirit intercedes with sighs too deep for words. And God, who searches the heart, knows what is the mind of the Spirit, because the Spirit intercedes for the saints according to the will of God.
>
> Romans 8:26–27.

To walk in prophetic intercession is sure to take you to new places in your experience with God. Some of those places will present a challenge to what has been comfortable before. There is a risk involved. Andy watched with interest. Jane was ministering to a young woman lying prostrate on the floor. The young woman was in evident discomfort and inner pain. She wept uncontrollably and occasionally thrashed around on the floor. The whole time Jane continued to pray quietly and authoritatively.

The strange thing was that two other women in different parts of the church building were exhibiting the same behaviour as the girl receiving ministry. When she screamed, they screamed. As she wept, they wept. And yet they were out of eyesight, both of the girl and of each other. Andy walked over to one of the women and asked if she knew what was happening. She commented haltingly that she was in intercession and prayer for the young woman Jane was ministering to. Andy approached the other prostrate girl and asked the same question. The reply which came back was that this young spiritual warrior was feeling the inner pain of the girl receiving ministry. After some time the young woman found peace as Jane continued in the Spirit. At that point the two who were praying also found peace. They were engaged in prophetic intercession.

Holly* and Barbara* were praying together. It was already the early hours of the morning, but both felt that they were touching something close to the heart of God. Quite suddenly, Holly felt an immense burden for a colleague who was going through some difficult circumstances. It was a situation of compounded grief with added complications. It had resulted in deep depression. Immediately the two of them interceded and prophesied with groaning and weeping as they felt something of their friend's pain. It was a depth of intercession they had not touched before, and continued for much of the night. God turned their friend's situation around in an amazing way. She came through the difficult time all the more strengthened for having passed through it. Holly and Barbara knew it could only be an answer to their prayers.

For some time we hosted renewal meetings in the community room of an apartment complex. One Tuesday evening, during a renewal meeting with folk from many different denominations, quite suddenly the direction of the meeting changed as we felt an urgency to pray for those living in the surrounding flats. We started to pray and as we did the Holy Spirit revealed to several a little of God's heart for those who did not know him as Father. Approximately a third of those present started to weep and moan, and some of them dropped to the floor as they interceded for those living nearby. It was a powerful move of the Spirit, not pre-planned by those leading the meeting.

In our experience roughly a third of people are burdened to

intercede in this way. However, as with all God's gifts, this is not an élitist thing. Those gifted in prophetic intercession are not 'more spiritual'. As we seek to walk a prophetic lifestyle we need each other. In one meeting three or four people were huddled together feeling a great weight of intercession. In another part of the meeting hall a woman, who had felt nothing of the weight, suddenly 'knew' what was on God's heart. She walked to the intercessors and revealed God's burden to them, then walked away. The weeping and moaning immediately increased as their prayers took on a new direction. We all need each other as we follow a prophetic lifestyle.

Father, what do you feel?

Prophetic intercession involves seeking to know what God feels about a situation we are praying about. It is not so much praying what we would like or desire but to receive revelation as to God's direction.

Of the many times we have experienced this, one time stands out. It occurred during 'The Watch of the Lord', an all-night Friday prayer vigil which we were keeping with about thirty other folk. We were praying around the church building we were meeting in, anointing significant parts of the building with oil in the name of the Lord and asking God for his revelation.

We decided to walk around the perimeter of the building. It was just after 3.00 am and we expected to be met by pitch blackness. The building is pretty much out in the country with no street lights. Instead, we found ourselves on a very bright moonlit night. It was so striking that we began to ask the Lord if the brightness of the night was in some way speaking of his good purposes for the church—that the night was over, light was shining. Almost immediately, as we prayed a bird began to sing beautifully and melodically. As we walked around the building the bird followed us, probably some twenty metres away but continuing its haunting lyric. It seemed to confirm to us that God was looking with favour on his church. As we walked and prayed the sound of a nearby stream came to us. We believed God was speaking about his river of life which was flowing among his people. We thanked him and prayed further. Around the back of the building we passed a large 'skip' full of rubbish. We paused to seek the Father and pray. He spoke about the rubbish and dross that he was purging from his people. We prayed fervently that God would throw out all of the garbage from his church! We passed hidden doorways and prayed for entrances to the family of God to be open and clear, and for dark forces to find no way of entry. By the windows we saw light streaming through and perceived that God was speaking of the light that shines from his church to the world. We accepted the revelation and prayed that the light would intensify. After about fifteen minutes we arrived back at the door by which we had left the building. 'Jane, my feet are soaking wet!' Andy complained. 'So are mine,' came the reply. We realised that the early morning dew was already falling on the ground.

'Lord, just as this dew saturates the whole of this estate, let your Spirit saturate your people who worship here,' was our final prayer. We rejoined our friends inside, thankful that the Father was teaching us to listen to his voice and to intercede by his revelation.

CHAPTER 11

YOU CAN ALL LIVE PROPHETICALLY

In our reading of the Celtic saints we are convinced that many of them lived a prophetic lifestyle. They listened to God. They perceived his voice in the circumstances of life and in creation. They were deeply intuitive. It has become our conviction that such a lifestyle is for all God's people, not just a select few.

Cuthbert had determined to enter the monastery at Melrose under the leadership of Boisil. Boisil was renowned for his holiness and virtue. By chance, Boisil was at the monastery gates when Cuthbert arrived. He had an immediate spiritual intuition that Cuthbert would be greatly used by God. To the assembled monks he said simply, 'Behold, the servant of the Lord!' In later years the monks realised the full import of the prophetic word.[44]

We have all been awestruck from time to time when we have heard a minister with the gift of prophecy calling out the particular and detailed needs of certain people in a congregation. How does she or he do that? What is the dynamic operating here? There is something of mystery about it all.

In the 1980s John Wimber in many ways demystified the healing ministry for us. God had been graciously restoring the gifts to his church. Healings had taken place, sometimes in remarkable ways. But in our experience there was still little teaching on the 'mechanics' of praying for sick people—'the how-do-you-do-this' type of approach. The same questions had exercised John Wimber's mind and over the years he had developed a model of praying for people which enabled many to exercise the gift of healing.[45]

Questions were asked like, 'How do you know when the Holy Spirit is present?', 'What do you look for?', 'Should I keep my eyes open or shut?', 'Is it all right to talk to someone in the middle of prayers?' etc. For some, this made the healing ministry too 'ordinary'. For us, and our guess is for many thousands more, it made it possible for anyone within the church to pray for the sick. It became very liberating. A good friend of ours once put it this way, 'We were already charismatic, but John Wimber demystified the healing ministry for us. Before it was just those with a special healing anointing. Now we can all pray and see God at work in our friends and families.'

The prophetic has had a similar kind of mystical shroud around it. Many of us have believed in prophetic ministry for some time. God does speak directly and immediately to the church. But many average church members, longing to hear God speak, are still unsure about it. Waiting week by week for a loud voice from heaven audibly addressing them, giving a certainty beyond doubt, just doesn't seem to work. 'Perhaps God only speaks to certain people, and probably not me!' The apostle Paul's conviction was somewhat different. 'For you can all prophesy one by one, so that all may learn and all be encouraged' (1 Corinthians 14:31). If that's true, how do we hear? What are the nuts and bolts of a prophetic lifestyle?

Listening to God . . . impressions

A favourite hymn for many of us will always be 'Dear Lord and Father of mankind, forgive our foolish ways'. It amused us in a marriage counselling class when one very-much-in-love couple wanted it as the opening hymn at their wedding service! Quite simply, it was their favourite hymn and held many associations for them. The softness and beauty of the melody linked with the words of 1 Kings 19 'O still small voice of calm'—have nourished and given comfort to generations of God's people.

The story of Elijah as God passed by on Mount Horeb has been used in many contexts. It remains one of the most evocative of all Bible passages: a great wind splitting the mountain and breaking rocks in pieces. Surely that was the voice of God? Not in these circumstances, though it was in others. Then a terrible earthquake. God must surely speak through such a great wonder of nature. On some occasions yes, but not this time. Then a fire. Now we know that 'our God is a consuming fire,' or as Eugene Peterson translates it, 'God himself is fire'. There must be a revelation in the fire. Not today! The terrible signs which Elijah witnessed were the very ones present when God gave the law to Israel, at the very same place. Then God was heard. On this day God was not speaking through the great signs of nature. The voice of God was in a still small voice.

We are convinced that at times God will speak through the great sign, the visible demonstration (we have said as much in other parts of this book), but we would want to add that the most frequent way God speaks to us in the body of Christ today is through the inner voice, the voice of the Spirit. The great signs, the portents and the wonders of God seem to be given to arrest our attention. The strange and unusual causes us to stop what we are doing. God is near. 'Lord, you now have our attention. Speak by your Spirit to our spirit whatever you want to say.'

It is that inner voice we want to explore in this chapter. How do we hear it? Mostly it will be in the form of some impression or other. We know of those who have heard what amounts to an audible voice, but this has been a very infrequent experience. In learning to walk in a prophetic lifestyle we need to become aware of the various impressions that God will bring to us mentally, emotionally, spiritually and physically. Learning how to interpret the impressions we receive will help us hear the voice of God more clearly.

God speaks to the mind

Thankfully, God is restoring to us a new understanding of the wholeness of human life. We are thinking *and* feeling people. We have perceptions, intuitions and abstract senses—and God uses all these as well as our thinking abilities. There is more of God to know and experience than ever we can fathom with our minds. To maintain correct doctrine does *not* guarantee a knowledge of God!

But that is not to say that we can ignore the mind. The ability to think and reason and work through logically is what in many ways separates us from the animals. The very fact that you are reading this page indicates a large degree of mental preparation and training, which is a great gift from God. And God will undoubtedly communicate with our minds. Paul wrestles with this whole complex of ideas in 1 Corinthians 14. He speaks of praying and speaking 'in the spirit' and 'with the mind' (verse 15). Both are good uses of God's gifts and he urges us to seek both expressions of our faith in Jesus.

In learning to hear God in our minds we want to suggest a few pointers. There will, of course, be times when God speaks to us through our rationality. Times when we meditate on the Scriptures, think through things, weigh things up and try to understand. It is said of C.S. Lewis that his most profound times with God were spent in reading a good book with pencil and pipe in hand, scribbling away as he wrestled in his thoughts with some truth or mystery of importance. Many such times will end with 'I still don't quite get it'. Other times will result in a kind of 'Eureka!' experience. 'Now I understand. It has just become clear to me.' Those who studied mathematics at school will remember the feeling when an algebraic formula made sense for the first time and the equation could at last be worked through to satisfactory completion. Having 'seen' it, we wonder how we ever missed it before.

We need to realise that God communicates in that way through our rational processes. To say 'I believe God spoke to me about . . . ' need not necessarily be a non-rational experience. Revelation comes through thought processes and just because it is so does not mean that we look down on it as some inferior kind of revelation.

But there are other ways God will communicate with the mind. God addresses the mind through dreams and visions and pictures. In some ways this is a 'right brain, left brain' distinction. Some of us are more suited to rational, cognitive, conceptual and 'wordy' uses of the mind. Others prefer to 'see' things with their minds. For them, truly, a 'picture is better than a thousand words'. Neither is better than the other and whatever our particular 'bent' it is useful to try to develop the other side of our character.

We, Jane and Andy, are both in many respects 'thinking' people and deal most easily with words, concepts and ideas. In attempting to live a prophetic lifestyle we are engaging facets of our personalities which have been pretty dormant! It's been good for us.

'Hi, Andy. It's Cathy. I think I've had a vision. It may have been a dream. I'm not sure. Get Jane and I'll share what happened.' Jane picked up another phone and we listened together and tried to make sense of our friend's phone call.

Cathy was at a conference and had fallen under the power of the Spirit. She wasn't sure whether she was awake or not. She couldn't say how long she was in this state, but in her mind's eye she saw a remarkable vision before her eyes. As she described it, it involved movement, extremely bright colours, and made such a strong impression that she felt she needed to phone long distance to speak to us about it. Briefly, it was a vision of a bird with very bright colourful wings evidently enjoying itself by a beautiful shoreline, with a sunny and transparently blue sky overhead. The whole scene was one of warmth, goodness and well-being. The scene changed dramatically as a large dark bird came into the picture, flew down and actually killed the smaller, colourful bird. The scene moved from light and well-being to darkness and destruction. It made a very powerful and disturbing impression on Cathy's mind.

We received her 'vision', thanked her for sharing it, told her not to worry (she had a distinct feeling it might be something bad) and set about praying. We also shared the vision with a few friends. Our collective interpretation was that there was an imminent spiritual attack—on us, our ministry or the renewal meetings we were a part of. We had already begun to learn that headaches, sudden illnesses and outward circumstances beyond our control were a part of spiritual warfare. Our prayers turned to ones of spiritual defence, seeking the armour of God and releasing the light of God in situations he brought to mind.

What the attack was we were never too sure on this occasion. After the event we believed that God had spoken, given warning to us and through our obedience in prayer we interrupted an attack of the enemy.

Cathy's experience helps us see how God communicates. Besides the rational process of the mind, God will give mental impressions to us. For simplicity's sake, a dream would be a 'moving picture', impressed on our mind while we are asleep. A vision would be the same kind of experience while awake, perhaps resting in the Spirit or in some situation where we 'day-dream' (not always a bad thing, though most certainly so in class!). A picture would be a mental impression which has no movement.

In a renewal meeting in a city in the Southern Tier of New York State, after a young woman, named Janet, had given her testimony she received prayer. She did not fall to the ground as others had done who had similarly received prayer that night. She just stood there. In fact she stood there right through the sermon and probably for an hour and a half into the time for prayer ministry later. She stood unmoved, and unmovable! Later, when we asked her if she knew what God was doing within her as she received prayer and waited in his presence, she told us, 'Oh, yes! God gave me a picture that was so clear. It was of a tree standing by a great river. The roots of the tree went deep underground and received all the nourishment it needed from the river. It was a very clear picture. Then the Lord spoke to me. He said that I was like that tree, planted by the river of life and that all that I needed came from him alone. I couldn't have moved even if I wanted to! I was planted in God.'

Though in both the above stories, we moved into interpretation of the impressions received (an important part of the process of hearing God, as we considered in a previous chapter) we want to emphasise at this point that *God speaks using impressions given to our minds.* Those impressions might be right or left-brain activities—reasoning and conceptual or concrete and pictorial. In either case we need to learn to listen to the impressions which come to us day by day and seek God for understanding and discernment of his voice.

Empathetic feeling

Andy realised that Janet had begun to cry. It was partly expected, not because Janet was necessarily prone to weeping in public, but because Janet, her husband John and Andy were part of a very moving celebration of holy communion involving some several thousand people. However, Janet did not stop weeping. Andy asked God to bless Janet. She cried further.

After an hour or so he asked, 'Janet, are you OK?'

'No,' she replied, 'Can't you see him?'

Andy scanned the vast crowd and looked somewhat bemused. 'See who?' he replied lamely.

'That man on the platform. He doesn't know the Lord and I am weeping for him.'

The man she pointed to was one of a large crowd gathered on the platform. Janet continued to cry for the next few hours. Trying to work through what had happened we realised later that God had shown Janet something very powerful; not through her mind but through her feelings. God had given her an empathy for a man she had never met and she began to feel deeply for the unsaved man in a way which reflected the way God felt for him. Her tears were tears of intercession.

God communicated to her through a very strong emotional impression.

It seems that God will use emotions in two ways. One is to allow someone to feel as he feels about a situation. (Of course, we realise that it can only ever be a partial revelation of God's heart. To truly feel all he feels would crush the human spirit.) In the move of the Spirit in the 1990s, intercession seems to have shifted from a mere 'list-of-things-to-pray-for' to feeling the heart of God for his world. God is communicating the way he feels for his church and world and releasing many in intercession in new ways.

Anne regularly prophesies in different languages. She is fluent in German, French, Russian and Welsh as well as English. We have been with her when the Holy Spirit moves powerfully. Anne 'switches' language and begins to think in a different tongue. She begins to 'see' a nation or part of a nation and then begins to feel as God does for that situation. We were talking with Anne and Dorothy. Without much warning we realised we were in God's presence and Anne began to prophesy in French concerning Algeria and the persecution of Christians there. She had not been speaking long when Dorothy began to weep. Dorothy had begun to 'feel' for the people of Algeria, in a small way as God does. It was a communication of God's heart, a revelation of his love and how his heart was breaking. Dorothy was heartbroken for some time as she interceded for that nation. She confessed she felt dreadful. Algeria had never been at the forefront of Dorothy's consciousness before. She was surprised by the deep reaction.

We will probably never know what situation was taking place at that moment far away across two seas, nor the effect that Anne and Dorothy's prayers had. It will be revealed in eternity. What we do believe is that through their sensitivity to hearing God at the level of their feelings, they were used by him to fulfil some part of his eternal plan for the world. Something as small as an inner impression can have a large effect in the purpose of God.

The second way that God uses our emotions is to allow us to feel as another human being feels. In this way he reveals to us their inner emotional need in order for us to pray or to help them in some way. We have often observed this in praying for people. Sometimes an overwhelming feeling of sadness envelops us. It is not our sadness. It doesn't relate to anything about us. God is allowing us to feel what the other person feels, in what amounts to a truly God-given empathy. It is a communication we can use in assuring the person we pray with that God knows what they feel. We can use it to pray more specifically, having been given insight. At the very least it produces a humility and sensitivity which helps us respect the other as an individual deeply loved by the Father and whose need he will meet.

Great sensitivity is needed in this area. Emotions are very fragile and we must be jealously careful in guarding the feelings of others. We have learnt that when God reveals to us the way others are feeling, and sometimes even the reason for their feeling, we must always pray in a respectful way. It must be in a way in which the other can reject what we say for we could well be wrong. Advice we gratefully picked up from the ministry training at the Toronto Airport Christian Fellowship was always to turn words of knowledge or wisdom or empathetic feelings into a prayer.

Jane was praying for someone. She received a revelation that the woman before her had been abused in the church and that it was the men in the church who had done so. It was a very strong sense and would clearly need sensitive handling whether it was right or wrong. At an appropriate time Jane prayed, 'Father, if your daughter has suffered hurt in your church, would you lift it from her.' By the physical effect this produced upon the woman as she stood for prayer, Jane realised that her discernment was correct. She prayed further, 'And Father if any of that abuse was from men in the church, in your mercy would you bring healing.' The prayer had hardly been uttered when the woman collapsed in a heap on the floor, sobbing deeply as God in answer to prayer began a deep healing in her life.

When God brings revelation to us, in whatever way, it is always to help, heal, encourage or bless one of his children. We need great sensitivity in the way we use the privilege of his communication. Indeed, the greater the sensitivity and the more humility we show, the more God will entrust to us. God 'resists the proud and gives grace to the humble'.

Someone has a problem with their lower back . . .

At times God will also communicate through physical means. This is somewhat hard to grasp as for the most part, in the West, we have had an uneasy relationship with our bodies! There has been a strong tradition that evil resides in the physical realm and that true spirituality is in some way or other to get out of the body.

The Scriptures are much more earthy than a great deal of our tradition. 'The earth is the Lord's and all its fullness' the Bible proclaims. Though presently tainted with sin, the body is still part of God's good creation and one day will be fully redeemed to resemble the body of Jesus. God is restoring a new sense of the goodness of our human bodies with all their capabilities and capacities. In renewal we have been put in touch with our bodies in new ways as in the presence of God many have sensed him physically as they have lost physical strength, laughed, cried, jerked, jumped or rolled!

God will also use our bodies to reveal his ways. On one occasion, we were to speak at a meeting for leaders and elders at a weekend retreat. As we were driving through the beautiful, tree-lined, Pennsylvanian countryside we were praying that God would speak to us prophetically. We wanted our ministry to be up-to-date and relevant. Suddenly Andy felt a sharp pain in his chest. The pain began as we were praying and we wondered if the Lord was speaking prophetically? The pain remained for most of the afternoon and during the ministry time Andy shared tentatively the unease he was feeling physically. 'It might be that there is someone here who has a heart condition. It may be physical but it may also speak about a broken heart that needs God's healing.' Amazingly, over fifty per cent of those present responded. A significantly high proportion of these leaders had physical heart complaints. As we prayed for healing the prophetic word increased and we perceived that God was also speaking about the 'heart of the church'. The ministry was well received. By the end of the session Andy no longer felt the pain.

Here we do need to add a word of caution! Please do not hesitate to seek medical opinion for any physical condition. We need to exercise a great deal of care and responsibility about this kind of word of knowledge. There is a need for both common sense and spiritual discernment. In our experience, and that of others we have talked to, once the prophetic word is spoken the physical symptom will disappear. But sometimes a back pain may be just that—a back pain! Get prayer by all means but also consult a doctor if symptoms persist (as all the medical advertisements say!).

Yet sometimes God may well be communicating to you. Our son Ben, while playing in the worship band, suddenly had a severe migraine headache. He had listened to our teaching on prophetic matters and confidently spoke out the word, 'Has anyone got a severe headache? We will pray for you right now.' And then with less boldness, 'And if there is no one, will someone please pray healing for me!' In the event two people responded for prayer and Ben's headache disappeared. He went back to playing his piano.

Learning from others

Randy, a British Anglican minister, has powerful gifts of healing accompanied by the word of knowledge. He will often receive revelation from God experienced as a physical sensation in some part of his own body.

Randy shared with us a couple of his many experiences. On one occasion, while ministering in York, he experienced a pain behind his kneecap. He was sure that this was God communicating with him prophetically. Randy spoke out the word of knowledge, and immediately there was a response. The gentleman who came forward shared that earlier that day a friend had told him he needed to get prayer for his knee. He had come to the meeting expecting to be healed!

Sometimes there is progressively increasing discernment. On another occasion Randy experienced a pain in his right cheek and eye. He shared that he believed it was a word of knowledge from God about a physical condition of someone present. As no one responded, Randy prayed further and received additional discernment that perhaps a black eye was involved. There was no response and Randy prayed further. The word of knowledge increased and Randy was able to say that it was a woman and that it involved a bicycle accident. This time a woman responded, finally confident that the word was for her! She received her healing.

The Information Superhighway, we are sure, is a gift from God. We have made many new friends over the Internet. Although we haven't seen many of these people face to face, we have shared our thoughts and many of our experiences with each other. Teresa shared the following story with us about how God gave her prophetic insight through the use of physical symptoms.

She had been ill all week, starting with a severe headache on Tuesday. By Thursday, Teresa was also experiencing pain in the kidney area and lower back. She was considering seeking medical advice, but decided to go to the Friday night renewal meeting just to receive prayer. Normally she served on the prayer ministry team but felt too ill to minister that evening. However, Teresa did join the ministry team to intercede for the meeting. She mentioned to others that she hoped the direction of the evening would be for healing. She discovered that others had also been experiencing similar physical symptoms during the week. The associate pastor suggested that these may be words of knowledge. During the prayer time these were released and many received powerful ministry. That night Teresa slept pain-free as the symptoms disappeared with the release of the prophetic word.

I know because I know because I know

On one occasion, Cuthbert was in Carlisle being shown around a remarkable Roman fountain. Some distance to the north a battle was being fought between Ecgfrith, King of Northumbria, and the Picts. Suddenly, Cuthbert was disturbed by a strong spiritual impression. He leaned heavily on his staff, sighed deeply and looked towards the sky. He shared with his friends the intuition that the battle had at that moment been decided. It proved to be so.[46]

There is a faculty we may term spiritual intuition. It is the most difficult to speak of because it is by far the deepest aspect of our beings and often defies neat andtidy categories. More often than not it is dismissed as something less than the rational, the rational always being considered superior. If it cannot be understood how can it have any value? We have to a large extent created a culture which places human reason at the pinnacle of human experience. To the extent we ignore the spiritual dimension of life, to that extent we are truly in poverty.

When people speak of 'feminine intuition' it is usually in a derogatory manner. Indeed, it may well be true that intuition is close to the feminine side of human make-up. Male arrogance has missed a great deal in looking down on this gift of God! In moral philosophy 'intuitionism' (the idea that morality can be known through some inner sense, apart from a rational explanation) is always viewed as inferior to other forms of ethics. In the Western liberal tradition human reason would dictate a duty based (Kant) or utilitarian (Bentham) ethic which the reasonable human being would both understand and agree to. Intuition is inherently unreliable. Yet, in seeking the mind of God we need the humility to move beyond our own powers of reason and to seek an intuition given Spirit to spirit. It will often be in the form of an inner check or confirmation. 'That's it. Do that. Don't do that.' The inner 'yes' and 'amen' of God is often a fleeting impression like the gentle breeze felt but difficult to grasp hold of.

Indeed, it is this spiritual intuition which undergirds the

other ways God speaks. Mind, emotion and body depend on the communication of God Spirit to spirit. It is the Spirit which enlightens the mind, activates the feelings and enlivens the body.

Most frequently the question is asked, 'How do you know?', and the answer is the nearly always unsatisfactory, 'I just know!' We desire a reason to know. We have been educated and encultured to look for a proof for our understanding, but in the things of God there is an element of mystery and gift. The sooner we come to terms with that fact the sooner we begin to walk close with God.

We are not, of course, suggesting the kind of closed-minded bigotry which crashes on regardless of others and assumes that no one else can lay claim to truth. Nor that having once been enlightened that we become unteachable and intransigent. Indeed, to walk close with God in the Spirit demands a humility of heart and mind which more gladly defers to others and seeks to learn from God from many sources. Clearly, our intuitions in the Spirit need to be tested and we want to explore that a little in the next chapter.

CHAPTER 12

TESTING PROPHETIC LIFESTYLE

Over the top, perhaps?

As we have shared about prophetic lifestyle in different settings in both the UK and USA we have observed two kinds of reaction. Some people are open mouthed and begin to share from their own experience the times when they have heard God speak in many and diverse ways. There is a resonance with their own experience. Indeed, some of the stories we have included were told to us after we had shared about prophetic lifestyle with others. Many are walking this way and have not labelled it as such. For many folk it has also opened up new ways of seeing God and experiencing his presence.

Another reaction is that it is all just too much! Some people are incredulous and the whole notion of daily finding God is dismissed as fanciful. It all sounds too risky. The unstable will use the ideas we have suggested as a way to become even 'weirder'! We are, of course, aware that in all these areas there is the danger of 'going over the top'. Indeed, if any of us were to seek God *only* in the realm of inner impression we would be in danger of leaving a safe path. We want to suggest a number of safeguards.

Deeply committed to the Scriptures

Celtic Christian communities were deeply committed to the Scriptures. Each day, during the Daily Office, the words of the Psalms and Gospels were read aloud and sank deeply into their consciousness. Celtic spirituality is full of allusions to the Scriptures.

Anyone who wants to take an inner journey, who wants to live in immediate communication with our Father, needs to be deeply committed to the Scriptures. Inner impressions or revelations from God will never in any circumstance show something contrary to the Scriptures and the more we know the truth of God revealed in the word of God the less likely we will be to fall into error. In fact, the more you know the Scriptures the more likely it will be that God will 'quicken' them and use them by way of direct revelation to your heart, mind and spirit. It is always interesting to read the writings of those who place a great emphasis on the inner life to see that their writings are permeated with references to the Scriptures. It is as if the light of scripture and the inner light of the Spirit fuse together to produce a wholeness and beauty.

We are committed to a serious approach to the Bible. It is not sufficient merely to brandish the text in any manner we desire. There are a number of approaches to understanding the text which will repay careful study and which will inform the inner journey. Demanding study is an important part of discipleship. Systematic theology (seeking a systematic and logical analytical treatment of the whole Bible), biblical theology (which looks at the Scriptures more in terms of the kind of writing, the unity and diversity of the text), narrative theology (taking the great stories and sweeping themes: creation, fall, redemption, captivity and release, birth, death and resurrection) all have their place. Historical theology is also important: seeing the great moves of God in history and how those in previous generations dealt with their experiences in the light of Scripture is most helpful to us now. All of this is important. When the dynamic of prophetic lifestyle is added to a mature understanding of the Scriptures something powerful and godly is given birth. Living with a deep love of the written word will help us make sense of the experienced word and keep us close to the right path.

Accountability in the body

There is also a sense that the prophetic lifestyle can only truly be lived in the safety of community. There is a great need for accountability within the family of God. In 1 Corinthians 14:29, Paul writes of one prophetically speaking (bringing revelation) and the other weighing what is said. The body of Christ is a safe place for the discernment the Spirit gives. Paul's message is clear—don't be a loose cannon! Don't be a lone ranger! If what you have received is truly beneficial then don't be afraid to share it with others in the family. But equally, be prepared for what you have received to be found wanting in some way. Simply because we have perceived something to be of God does not necessarily mean it is. In fact, we must be prepared for a certain amount of mixture in the things we receive. With maturity and practice there will be more accuracy, more clarity, but as we begin there is a great need to check things out, to put what we have before others and to be willing to be corrected. In the vulnerability of sharing we are prepared for a resounding 'Amen', a cautious 'Partly yes, partly no' and even a loving 'I think you may have got that wrong!'

In our teaching and equipping seminars on prophetic issues we encourage those who are seeking revelatory gifts to be accountable to the leadership of their churches. In whatever relationship of trust and submissiveness you are in, there must be an accountability. It is important to find out the ground rules and 'church etiquette' which apply in your fellowship. Some churches are very free flowing and anyone is given space to bring a word from God, share an insight or begin a prophetic song. Other churches are less free but still give space provided the church leader(s) give the go ahead. Still others find the whole revelatory ministry problematic and give little public space for sharing. Some prefer words to be written down and submitted for consideration. The permutations are many and varied! But it is important to know. Talk to your church leader, pastor, vicar or priest. Find out what is acceptable and work within it. Prophetic ministry is not meant to be rebelliousness fighting against the appointed leadership of the church.

Watching the tongue

Here is a golden rule—never allow your hearing from God to be a point of criticism of leaders in God's family. It's simply not your place to do so.

Of all the people on the earth, Noah found peculiar favour with God. His obedience is legendary—building a huge boat in the middle of the desert waiting for rain which had never been seen before. But like us all, Noah had his weak spot. Being a good entrepreneur he planted a vineyard. He learned the secret of producing wine and then became a victim of his own success—Noah was the first drunk recorded in the Bible!

He drank some of the wine and became drunk, and he lay uncovered in his tent. And Ham, the father of Canaan, saw the nakedness of his father, and told his two brothers outside Then Shem and Japheth took a garment, laid it on both their shoulders, and walked backward and covered the nakedness of their father; their faces were turned away, and they did not see their father's nakedness.

(Genesis 9:21–23)

The way his sons reacted is very instructive. Ham saw his father's drunken nakedness and began the gossip. Dad was in the wrong and others ought to know about it. Ham believed it was his duty to expose the error to others. Shem and Japheth took a different route. Rather than expose dad's nakedness, they covered it: they supported him, they were totally loyal.

Church leaders are all too fallible. Every once in a while even the best have their nakedness exposed for all to see. How do we react? Many of us adopt Ham's way and tell of the nakedness we see. Shem and Japheth took the more noble way: they covered the sin and protected their father's reputation. Be careful lest a prophetic lifestyle becomes a thin veil for the way of Ham!

King Saul also sinned. His wrong was sufficiently serious for the kingdom to be taken away from him. A new king would be chosen, anointed and given the authority to lead Israel. The new king was a young man called David. At God's command the prophet Samuel anointed David to be king while Saul was still on the throne. Saul, in his turn, did not want to give up the throne so easily. Over a long period of time he systematically persecuted David. Of interest to us is the way David reacted to Saul.

At this juncture Saul was still God's appointed leader of his people. David was in the wings but is not yet to enter centre stage. There is one interesting episode when Saul, weary from fighting the Philistines, sought rest in a roadside cave. Unbeknown to Saul, this was the very cave where David and his mighty warriors were also taking shelter. This was David's chance. The very man who had sought his life was now within striking distance, unarmed and away from his bodyguard. Some of the warriors urged David to strike the mortal blow. David merely cut the corner of Saul's cloak, but even that was inappropriate to do to God's appointed leader. His conscience was smitten and he told his men: '"The LORD forbid that I should do this thing to my lord, the LORD's anointed, to raise my hand against him; for he is the LORD's anointed." So David scolded his men severely and did not permit them to attack Saul. Then Saul got up and left the cave, and went on his way' (1 Samuel 24:6–7).

David, like Shem and Japheth, had learned a valuable lesson. He respected the leader of God's people and would not do harm to God's anointed, *even when the leader was in the wrong*. It's a lesson which is strange in many churches today where under the guise of democracy or 'concern for the church', pastors and leaders are too freely criticised, admonished and summarily fired by the people they serve. When prophetic ministry is used to buttress criticism of leadership the gift is misused.

Sadly, one of the worst effects of the restoration of the prophetic ministry to the church has been the self-elevation of those who think they hear God more clearly than anointed leaders in the church. By all means share your revelation with leaders, but give them freedom to act responsibly before God. They will often see a broader picture than you, and your revelation might be just one small piece of a larger jigsaw.

Occasionally someone says, 'Well, Jesus criticised the Pharisees. And Paul wrote strongly to the Corinthians and Galatians—even telling Peter off for his hypocrisy.' True enough. But neither you nor we are Jesus or Paul! If we have a ministry let it be upbuilding, humbly seeking God and out of a position of humility.

What about rejection?

Some readers will be uncomfortable with the last few paragraphs. Your mind will be protesting, 'It's all right for you to say that—but you don't know my church! Every prophetic insight is always rejected.'

We are not saying, of course, that church leaders are infallible or that folk are blindly to follow. But if you are part of a church where however much you try you cannot respect the leadership, or where the leaders are opposed to the moving of the Spirit of God, then you have a choice to make. If you are called to be part of that community then you need to pray and love and pray and love until God moves. If you are not called then you need to find the place of God's calling. There is no shame in moving on. But whichever path you take, criticism, gossip and using 'prophetic words' against others in the family of God is always inappropriate.

Rejection is a powerful emotion. If we do not deal with rejection it can easily become a root of bitterness which defiles us and others. It is very sad to see good people of God who have allowed rejection to eat away at their inner life. There are pastors rejected by the church who can only speak ill of the people of God. There are prophetic people rejected by their church who continue to carry the hurt, which shows through in all they say and do. Rejection can be a cancer which eats away at spiritual life with almost unstoppable ease. How do we deal with it? The key is in extending forgiveness to those who have rejected us. We need to free them from the debt which they owe us and give them over to the mercy of God. If you find it hard to do this on your own, find a trusted and mature believer with whom you can share and who will pray with you in the Spirit to unlock the bitterness and release you from it.

Finding a soul friend

That leads us to one particular area of accountability which we feel is most valuable. We strongly recommend that you find a soul friend, called an *anamchara* in the Celtic tradition, and in other traditions a 'spiritual director'.

> A young cleric of the community of Ferns, a foster-son of Brigit's, used to come to her with wishes. He was often with her in the refectory to partake of food. One time, after coming to commu- nion, she struck a bell. 'Well, young cleric there,' said Brigit, 'do you have a soul friend?'
>
> 'I have,' replied the young man.
>
> 'Let us sing his requiem,' said Brigit, 'for he has died. I saw when you had eaten half your portion of food that that portion was put in the trunk of your body, but that you were without any head. For your soul friend has died, and anyone without a soul friend is like a body without a head. Eat no more until you get a soul friend.[47]

To choose a soul friend is to develop a deeply personal relationship of trust and openness in which the life of faith is shared and through which we can grow. Intuitions, revelations and perceptions are shared with a soul friend to whom we voluntarily become accountable and responsible even to the point of correction. With much talk in the church about 'heavy shepherding' and the sad mistreatment of many by rigid sys- tems of authority, the question of accountability has been 'de- emphasised'. But there is an important truth in mutual submission (what theologian John Howard Yoder calls 'radical subordinationism') in the family of God.

If you are thinking of finding a soul friend there are a number of characteristics which might help you:

- The soul friend needs to be a mature believer who has walked with Christ for many years. He/she is familiar with the moving of the Spirit. It would be inappropriate to find someone who is opposed to the moving of the Spirit or is a stranger to the inner voice of God.
- The soul friend is implicitly trustworthy. Nothing that is shared in the context of an accountable relationship is shared outside of that relationship.
- The soul friend need not be from the same Christian tradition. There are very profitable relationships of free-church people whose spiritual directors are Catholics, Anglicans with house-church folk and other combinations. We have benefited greatly from those in other traditions who both challenge and stretch us in new directions.
- The soul friend need not be a minister nor does she need to be male!

If you are asked to be a soul friend these things may help:

- Be willing to keep confidences.
- Take sin seriously, but do not be judgmental or over-bearing.
- Seek the Lord as to how you may be like Jesus to your friend.
- Do not try to control your friend's life or manipulate according to your own agenda.

It is important to be humble and be a learner from others who have walked the path before you.

CHAPTER 13

LIVING WITH THE LOOSE ENDS

'Twenty years,' Jane remarked. 'I can hardly believe it!'

Twenty years is a long time. It's just under a third of our lives if we reach the 'three score and ten'. It's a quarter if we make it to the exclusive ranks of the octogenarians. Our closest friends had clubbed together to give us an unexpected treat and our twentieth wedding anniversary found us in a quiet little restaurant enjoying one another. It was a rare night out in a busy schedule.

We talked for hours of the many things we had shared together—the birth and growth of our children, the churches we had been a part of, the friends we had known, the odd grey hair that was just beginning to show through. So much had transpired. We were so grateful to God.

But imagine waiting twenty years for the fulfilment of some prophecy or other. As we began to live a prophetic lifestyle, from time to time we grew impatient. Surely if God has promised something it should happen pretty soon? Not necessarily so. We are beginning to learn to live with the loose ends.

It's particularly challenging for us because we are both the kind of people who like to see things neat and tidy. If we are engaged in a project we want to press through to a quick conclusion. His promise today may not be fulfilled tomorrow or even the day after.

In Chapter 1 we told of our trip to Toronto and the melting of the snow. That was not the end of the story. At Toronto that January we were given a prophetic word by a Christian friend from San Francisco. She told us that there would be a spiritual breakthrough . . . at Christmas! This was January, and Christmas was a year away! To be honest, after holding the word for a while we forgot about it. It meant another year of spiritual warfare. But just a week or so before Christmas, Kathleen e-mailed us to remind us of God's word of promise. It proved to be true. Christmas brought a new sense of anticipation and release in the Spirit.

Immediately after Christmas we felt constrained to pray about a renewal conference. The end of February/beginning of March seemed to be right and so we prayed. It was a little over six weeks away. We gathered for our Thursday morning prayer meeting. 'Lord, if you want us to have this conference, would you show us who you would like us to invite.' As the words were being prayed the phone rang.

'Hi Andy. It's Jim Paul calling from Toronto. I was just praying and God placed you on my heart. I have had a cancellation and wonder if you would like me to come and speak at a conference in Ithaca. The dates I have available are 27th February–1st March. I think the Lord wants to unstop the well of the Spirit!'

The immediacy of the answer to prayer was somewhat overwhelming. It felt somewhat like the disciples in Acts 12. Peter was in prison and his friends prayed desperately for his release. God answered through the intervention of an angel and Peter was set free. He knocked on the door of the room where the prayer meeting was in progress. His friends couldn't believe it was him. They were still praying for his release! We knew just a little of how they must have felt.

It was all the more significant in that it was Jim who had prophesied over us some twenty months previously about a 'well of spiritual renewal' in the Finger Lakes. Twenty months had seemed a long time, but we have discovered that our Father does not operate on the same time-scale that we do.

In the event, nearly 400 people registered for the conference and God was powerfully present throughout. Many people found a new release in the power of the Holy Spirit and further significant prophetic words were released about the move of God in New York. We await their further fulfilment. More loose ends!

Abraham, Sarah and the promise of Isaac

God made the most astonishing promises to Abram. He was not a young man. Abram was already seventy-five years old when God told him in Genesis 12 that he would have many descendants. 'That's great, God, when is the first child to be born?' Not for many years. Abram and Sarai had to learn to live with the loose ends.

There is a warning repeated a number of times in different ways in the story of Abraham and Sarah—we may fall into the trap of trying to tie up the loose ends ourselves. They found it as difficult as we do. Though God reiterated the call a number of times, both Abram and Sarai were not past trying to help God out. In Genesis 15 Abram suggested to the Lord that his slave Eliezer is his only heir. There appeared to be an element of impatience as Abram even wondered 'what good is the promise?' when there was no living heir. But Abram's suggestion about Eliezer was born from his impatience with the timing of prophetic fulfilment. In chapter 16 Abram tried to tie the loose ends further when Sarai suggested that Abram have sexual relations with the slave girl Hagar. At least then the child would be Abram's, even though not Sarai's. It was still not God's timing for the fulfilment of the promise. A son was born, but Ishmael, though blessed by God, became a stumbling block to the child of promise.

Abraham and Sarah lived with the loose end of God's promise until Abraham was one-hundred years old and Sarah well past the age of bearing children. Twenty-five years of waiting, holding the promise of God. During that time doubts would arise, 'Have we truly heard God?' Friends would question, 'Surely you can't still be holding onto that old promise?'

It seems to us that if we are to walk closely with God, hearing his communication, receiving his prophetic word each day, then living with loose ends is part and parcel of life. For all of us, at least for the time being, loose ends are God's agenda.

For Abraham and Sarah, the lesson was even clearer in that by the time of fulfilment there was no human possibility for the promise to be fulfilled. Sarah was past the age of child-bearing and Abraham was by then very old. It tells us that even our clear prophetic words from God may move beyond the 'sell-by date'. It is all a matter of God's timing and our learning.

Joseph and his family

We looked at Joseph the dreamer in Chapter 5. We want to return to his story because it helps us see something about living with the loose ends of a prophetic lifestyle. One of the problems Joseph faced was that even though his dreams were clearly from God and the interpretation plain, God's timing was an issue which Joseph took a long time to learn. The dreams were a true revelation of what was to follow and in God's time it would come to pass just as the dreams had foretold. But it didn't happen immediately. There is a long story of revenge by the brothers, being sold into slavery, the ignominy of prison, the false accusations of indecency, further prophetic interpretation of dreams and eventual rise to prominence in the great Egyptian empire. Finally, *after twenty years*, the dream is proven true as first the brothers and then accompanied by the parents the family bows before Joseph who had become the second most powerful man in Egypt. The dream would be fulfilled twenty years in the future.

The story is full of insight for us as we seek to live prophetically. It would have been better if Joseph had not shared the dreams in the first place. It brought him a lot of trouble and caused a divided family much heartache. When he disappeared it broke his father's heart. The next twenty years were agony for Jacob. The brothers for their part lived with a huge weight of guilt for the same period. In God's goodness and mercy the whole situation was turned around. Joseph himself realised that though his brothers had meant it for evil God had meant it for good. However, because God turned the situation around, we still cannot ignore the fact that Joseph acted unwisely in the first place.

Prophetic words are not always to be shared. We have come to realise that prophetic insight is often intended to help us in our prayers—seeking the face of God for what he has revealed. If Joseph had only hidden the revelation in his heart, prayed it through and acted with kindness towards the family who would one day bow down to him, things might well have been different. Undoubtedly, the dreams would have been fulfilled, but probably in a far different way.

In this we truly need wisdom from God. Some dreams and visions are to be held, waiting to see the Lord act. By all means write them down, date them, but hold onto them. Some words have been given to us personally which we are still holding, unwilling to share them yet as we wait for God's timing. It's quite possible that many of the things given to us as revelation will never be shared with anyone. They are deeply personal and secret intimacies between us and our Saviour.

Joseph's story teaches us that there might be a long period between prophetic revelation and fulfilment. What God whispers to us today may not be for today, or tomorrow or any time in the near future. His revelation may be pointing to the direction of our life which will find completion years into the future.

Partial revelation

Joseph's story also shows us that the whole picture is not revealed to us prophetically. To the seventeen-year-old the very thought of family members bowing down may have proved too heady. God had revealed where Joseph would one day be but he did not reveal the process by which Joseph needed to travel to be there. There were many rough edges that needed smoothing before all came to pass. God did not speak of the process of slavery, imprisonment and humiliation.

We have spent many happy weeks walking the Lake District hills in Cumbria. There is nothing as exhilarating as a stiff climb and the panoramic views given as a reward for labour as the summit is climbed. Looking from the top of Blencathra to the east of Keswick on a clear day you can see Helvelyn to the south and Skiddaw to the west. Beautiful, majestic mountains. Their very names conjure all kinds of romantic images. But often from the valley the tops of the hills are shrouded in mist. On some occasions it is the valleys themselves which cannot be seen. Looking from the top of one peak, the other high peaks appear as icebergs in a vast sea of mist. To get from one place to the next means descending into the valley where there is no clear vision. Sometimes God's revelation to us is as the peaks. He reveals Blencathra, Skiddaw, Helvelyn and that is our destination. But the process, the way to the peaks remains veiled. Valleys, trees, smaller hills, fences, stone walls, towns and villages, major and minor roads, lakes, rivers and streams all become part of the process.

More than once we have been lost. We have seen the peak. We know it is there. But in the valley all looks the same. The clouds hide the summit from view. In the mist we have doubted that we will ever really get to the top. At times it is hard to imagine it is even there. Was it merely a dream? To walk in the valley, to embrace the process is to learn to live with the loose ends.

Have a good prophetic shelf and journal!

We were once advised to make sure we have a good shelf in our consciousness. As we walk with Jesus there will be many times when we face things we do not understand, cannot fathom, even things that simply confuse us. Place those things on the shelf. It is not to deny them nor is it to pretend they are of no consequence. It is to say, with humility, that there are truly things we cannot now know and that there are true revelations from God which transcend our best attempts at explanation.

Over the last few years we have been given prophetic words from God which have been repeated a number of times in different settings by different people, but with much the same content. Some of them we have shared in the pages of this book. Many of them we haven't. Some are very personal and we doubt whether they will ever be shared in a public context. The ones we have included, we hope, will be able to give a 'feel' of what living prophetically can be like.

We are still waiting upon many words, impressions and visions from God. Our prophetic shelf has a good deal on it! We are still waiting for a further release and confirmation with regard to Native Americans in the place where we live. We are sure there are still painful memories to be healed, curses to be overcome and their is blood on the hands of European settlers in the USA. There is a need of deep reconciliation and we have seen just the beginning of it. The small work that we have seen is part of a larger strategy that God has to bring all things under Christ. We long for more.

We are also, as we write, waiting for the flood of God's blessing that has been promised, prophesied and dreamt about. We have seen great break-through. We have seen walls of defensiveness and division come down between pastors and churches. We have drunk deeply of the well of God. Snow has melted and we have enjoyed a springtime of sorts. But we know there is more: there is greater fulfilment yet to be.

One of the friends in our home church encapsulates living with loose ends. Danny is a creative musician who plays bass and is in the process of building a recording studio. He was brought up in a Christian home but, sadly, like so many young people, was turned off God by the political bickering in the church he belonged to. He walked away from God and found himself a part of the alternative punk culture of the late seventies and early eighties. However, deep inside, Danny still wanted to know God. One day he cried out to God in some desperation. His prayer was to the effect that if God loved him, would he provide Danny with a 'gig'. Three days later a man came to Danny and asked if he would play in a Christian band. Danny realised his foolishness for doubting God's goodness and asked his forgiveness. About that time, 1986, his pastor in Waikiki Hawaii prophesied over Danny that he would be greatly used as a bass player in the kingdom.

Nothing immediately came of the prophecy. Danny waited and during that time moved to New York. Ten years later, he found himself in a renewal meeting playing bass in a worship band exploring creative ways of playing together in the Spirit. A prophetic minister prophesied publicly that 'God wanted a bass player in heaven' and had found Danny. The prophecy continued that Danny would be involved in new and unique instrumental music. The word confirmed the prophecy of ten years before and unbeknown to the minister, Danny is near completing his first album of instrumental music in a new style which is a mixture of fusion, Jazz and techno. For Danny, some of the loose ends are coming together. But it has been a long process which still has some way to go. He is learning to live prophetically.

It may help to keep a record of the way God speaks to you. Some people have the ability to recall events, circumstances and happenings at will from the past. Most of us don't. Though an experience may seem very vivid today, in six months time we may lose much of its impact. In living prophetically it has helped us to keep a note of dates and words given, impressions received and the events of life. As you look back over time you will probably be able to discern some sort of pattern. You will see what things have been fulfilled and what things remain on the shelf. In years to come we are convinced you will have a story to tell of the way God has dealt with you and proved his love again and again.

The Celtic knot

There is a great mystery in following Jesus. Living prophetically—in the now of God's revelation and presence—is in many ways enigmatic. We want to end this book, but in truth there is no end!

Celtic knotwork is perhaps the clearest way of describing prophetic lifestyle. Have you ever been captivated by the intricacy and beauty of Celtic art? In our main living room we have a large banner with six depictions of the wild goose, the Celtic symbol of the Holy Spirit. The legs of each of the geese form the beginning of the intricate weave of a Celtic design. Guests to our home often spend a great deal of time relaxing and meditating on the beauty and intricacy of the theme. Where does it start? Where does it end? Where does each strand lead? Of course, in the design of the Celts is a great sense of the eternal. There is no beginning and no ending in eternity.

Ian Bradley, who uses the Celtic knot as a recurring motif in his *The Celtic Way,* summarises what the knotwork of the Celtic Christians depicts:

> It is full of suggestions of potentialities to be realised and possibilities to be encountered. Its progress is not easy or effortless—there are many detours and false trails to be pursued, and superimposed on the pattern is the Cross of suffering and sacrifice. But there is a sense of everything fitting together, of the intimate intertwining of the material and the spiritual, humans and nature, God and the world, the Cross and creation.[48]

What Bradley says of the Celtic knot we feel deeply about prophetic lifestyle. We are still not sure how we were led this way. We are sure, though, that we now have a greater sense of the immanence of a Father who loves us dearly and cares about us intimately. We know that he desires more than anything else to communicate with us through his Spirit. And we have discovered the joy and wonder of finding his speaking in all of life and circumstances. Our prayer is that you too may learn to live prophetically in the 'now' of the Father's revelation.

NOTES

1 Guy Chevreau, *Catch the Fire* (Toronto: Harper Collins, 1994).
2 Guy Chevreau, *Pray with Fire* (Toronto: Harper Collins, 1994).
3 In Celtic stories there are variations on a number of names. Columba is Columcille is Colum Cille is Crimmthan; Brid is Bridet is Bridget is Brigit; Hild is Hilda; Ita is Ide; David is Dewi.
4 If you wish to pursue a study of Celtic Christianity, the list for further reading at the back of this book will be a good place to start. For anyone who wishes to continue daily prayer in the Celtic tradition, either those books of prayer from David Adam or those of the Northumbrian community will be of great help. Of the many good books recently published on the Celtic church, we recommend Michael Mitton's *Restoring the Woven Cord* (London: Darton, Longman and Todd, 1995) as a good all-round introduction. Edward C. Sellners *Wisdom of the Celtic Saints* (Notre Dame: Ave Maria Press, 1993) is a good book of primary sources with some commentary. Elizabeth Culling has a good brief introduction *What is Celtic Christianity?* (Grove Booklet Series: Nottingham, 1993). Of course, David Adam, Vicar of Holy Island, has a series of excellent little books on Celtic spirituality. Most of these books have bibliographies to send the reader further afield.

5 Throughout this book we are using 'saint' in its more general sense of 'Christian' rather than specifically canonised saints.

6 Edmund, in C.S. Lewis's *The Lion, The Witch and the Wardrobe* (Macmillan: New York, 1950 edition), p 114.

7 Esther de Waal in her introduction to Helen Waddell, *Beasts and Saints* (London: Darton, Longman and Todd, 1995), p xxviii.

8 Written in the margin of a manuscript of the Latin grammarian Priscian, which was copied by Irish monks at St Gall in the first half of the ninth century. Old Irish, in Oliver Davies and Fiona Bowie, *Celtic Spirituality: An Anthology of Medieval and Modern Sources* (London: SPCK, 1995), p 29.

9 Alan Garner, *The Wierdstone of Brisingamen* (London: Lions, 1960, 1992) and *The Moon of Gomrath* (London: Collins, 1963, 1995).

10 In Leonard von Matt and Walter Hauser, tr. Sebastian Bullough, OP, *St Francis of Assisi* (Chicago: Henry Regnery Company, 1956), p 38.

11 Edward C. Sellner, *op. cit.*, (1993), p 61. A more complete account of Brendan can be found in D.H. Farmer, ed., *The Age of Bede* (Harmondsworth: Penguin Books, 1965), pp 211–245.

12 Steve Wall and Harvey Arden, *Wisdomkeepers: Meeting with Native American Spiritual Elders* (Hillsboro: Oregon: Beyond Words Publishing, 1990), pp 22–23.

13 Edward C. Sellner, *op. cit.*, pp 161–162.

14 In the foreword by F.F. Bruce to Clifford Hill, *Prophecy Past and Present* (Crowborough: Highland Books, 1989), pxii.

15 Eugene H. Peterson, *The Message, the New Testament and Psalms* (Colorado Springs: NavPress, 1994), p 20.

16 Don Richardson, *Eternity in Their Hearts* (Venture, CA: Regal Books, 1981, revised 1984).

17 Ian Bradley, *The Celtic Way* (London: Darton, Longman and Todd, 1993), p 6. Bradley suggests that this might be a reference to the notion of the eternal *Logos* present in every culture. He also suggests, following Karl Rahner, that in every culture there are 'anonymous Christians' who unconsciously worship Christ.

18 The story of Anne Hutchinson can be read more fully in Mark A. Noll, *A History of Christianity in the United States and Canada*

(Grand Rapids, MI: W.B. Eerdmans, 1992), pp 60–62. Also in Cotton Mather, *The Great Works of Christ in America*, Volume 2 (Edinburgh: The Banner of Truth Trust, 1979), pp 516–520.

19 The following all shed differing insights on the enigma of Joan of Arc. Polly Schoyer Brooks, *Beyond the Myth: The Story of Joan of Arc* (New York: Harper and Row, 1959). Frances Winwar, *The Saint and the Devil: Joan of Arc and Gilles de Rais* (New York: Harper and Brothers, 1948).

20 See, for example, the Anabaptist Pilgram Marpeck, 'On the Inner Church, 1545', in William Klassen and Walter Klassen, *The Writings of Pilgram Marpeck* (Scottdale, PA: Herald Press, 1978), pp 418–426.

21 *George Fox, an Autobiography,* edited with an Introduction and Notes by Rufus M. Jones.

22 Issued in modern translation by Gene Edwards as *Experiencing the Depths of Jesus Christ* (Gardiner, Maine: Christian Book Publishing House, 1975).

23 For further information on Jeanne Guyon, see T.C. Upham, *Life, Religious Opinions and Experiences of Madame Guyon* (London: Allenson and Co., Ltd., 1905).

24 Edward C. Sellner, *op. cit.*, pp 84–85.

25 *Ibid*, p 114.

26 For those who have a mind to delve further, perhaps the single most useful book we have found on hermeneutics is Willard Swartley's *Slavery, Sabbath, War and Women* (Scottdale, PA: Herald Press). Swartley's book is not always easy, but will repay careful study.

27 *After Virtue, A Study in Moral Theory* (London: Gerald Duckworth and Company, Ltd., second edition, 1985), p 212.

28 Please note that we are not endorsing the entire message of the film! In some respects the film reinforces what theoligian Walter Wink calls 'the myth of redemptive violence' which is told again and again in our culture: that the way to right wrongs is through violent means. See Walter Wink, *Engaging the Powers: Discernment and Resistance in a World of Domination* (Minneapolis: Fortress Press, 1992). That aspect of the *Braveheart* story is not one we would wish to uphold. We truly believe in the truth of redemp-

tive suffering, the cross of Christ, and not victory through hating and killing enemies.

29 Andy and Jane Fitz-Gibbon, *Something Extraordinary is Happening* (Crowborough: Monarch Publications, 1995), p 148.

30 Ray Crognale, *Awake O Knight* (1996).

31 For a fuller acount of the tale see Helen Waddell, *op. cit.*, pp 127–130.

32 Andrew Walker, *Telling the Story: Gospel, Mission and Culture* (London: SPCK, 1996), p 39.

33 David Adam has an excellent commentary on the prayer in *The Cry of the Deer* (London: SPCK/Triangle, 1987).

34 C.S. Lewis, *The Horse and His Boy* (Harmondsworth: Puffin, Penguin, 1954).

35 Peter L. Berger, *A Rumour of Angels* (Garden City, NY: Doubleday and Company, 1969).

36 Peter L. Berger, *The Heretical Imperative: Contemporary Possibilities of Religious Affirmation* (Garden City, NY: Doubleday, 1979).

37 Ian Bradley, *Columba: Pilgrim and Penitent* (Glasgow: Wild Goose Publications, 1996), p 79.

38 Edward C. Sellner, *op. cit.*, p 154.

39 *Celtic Daily Prayer: A Northumbrian Office* (London: Harper Collins, 1994) p 322.

40 *Ibid*, p 323.

41 Edward C. Sellner, *op. cit.*, pp 107–108.

42 Robert Van de Weyer, *Celtic Fire* (London: Darton, Longman and Todd, 1990).

43 The use of * indicates that we have changed the name at the person's request.

44 See D.H. Farmer, ed., *op. cit.*, p 50.

45 See John Wimber and Kevin Springer, *Power Healing* (London: Hodder and Stoughton, 1986).

46 See D.H. Farmer, *op. cit.*, pp 77–78.

47 Edward C. Sellner, *op. cit.*, p 73.

48 Ian Bradley, *The Celtic Way* (London: Darton, Longman and Todd, 1993), pp 68–69.

FOR FURTHER READING

We have found the following books useful in trying to understand prophetic lifestyle.

On the Celtic Christian tradition:

Adam, David, *The Edge of Glory. Prayers in the Celtic Tradition* (London: Triangle/SPCK, 1985); *The Eye of the Eagle. Meditations on the Hymn 'Be Thou my Vision'* (London: Triangle/SPCK, 1990); *The Cry of the Deer. Meditations on the Hymn of St Patrick* (London: Triangle/SPCK, 1987); *The Rhythm of Life. Celtic Daily Prayer* (London: Triangle/SPCK, 1996).

Bradley, Ian, *The Celtic Way* (London: Darton, Longman and Todd, 1993); *Columba Pilgrim and Penitent* (Glasgow: Wild Goose Publications, 1996).

Carmichael, Alexander, *New Moon of the Seasons* (Edinburgh: Floris Books, 1982).

Culling, Elizabeth, *What is Celtic Christianity?* (Bramcote: Grove Booklets, 1993).

De Waal, Esther, *The Celtic Way of Prayer: The Recovery of Religious Imagination* (London: Hodder and Stoughton, 1996).

Davies, Oliver, and Bowie, Fiona, *Celtic Christian Spirituality, An Anthology of Medieval and Modern Sources* (London: SPCK, 1995).

Farmer, D.H., *The Age of Bede* (London: Penguin, 1965).

Mitton, Michael, *Restoring the Woven Cord, Strands of Celtic Christianity for the Church Today* (London: Darton, Longman and Todd, 1995).

The Northumbria Community, *Celtic Daily Prayer* (London: Marshall Pickering, 1994); *Celtic Night Prayer* (London: Marshall Pickering, 1996).

Sellner, Edward C., *Wisdom of the Celtic Saints* (Notre Dame: Ave Maria Press, 1993).

Simpson, Ray, *Exploring Celtic Spirituality: Historic Roots for Our Future* (London: Hodder and Stoughton, 1995).

Van de Weyer, Robert, *Celtic Fire, an Anthology of Celtic Christian Literature* (London: Darton Longman and Todd, 1990).

Waddell, Helen, *Beasts and Saints* (London: Darton, Longman and Todd, 1995).

Whiteside, Lesley, *The Spirituality of Saint Patrick*, Blackrock, County Dublin: The Columba Press, 1996).

On prophetic things generally:

Bickle, Mike, *Growing in the Prophetic* (Eastbourne: Kingsway, 1995).

Cooke, Graham, *Developing Your Prophetic Gifting* (Tonbridge: Sovereign World, 1994).

Grudem, Wayne, *The Gift of Prophecy* (Eastbourne: Kingsway, 1988).

Hamon, Bill, *Prophets and Personal Prophecy* (Shippensburg, PA: Destiny Image, 1987); *Prophets, Pitfalls and Principles* (Shippensburg, PA: Destiny Image, 1991); *Prophets and the Prophetic Movement* (Shippensburg, PA: Destiny Image, 1990).

Hill, Clifford, *Prophecy Past and Present* (Crowborough: Highland, 1989).

Hill, Clifford and Monica, . . . *And They Shall Prophesy!* (London: Marshall Pickering, 1990).

Joyner, Rick, *The Harvest* (Springdale, PA: Whittaker House, 1979, 1983); *The Final Quest* (Charlotte, NC: Morning Star Publications,

1996); *Overcoming Racism* (Charlotte, NC: Morning Star Publications, 1996); *Overcoming The Accuser* (Charlotte, NC: Morning Star Publications, 1996); *Overcoming Witchcraft* (Charlotte, NC: Morning Star Publications, 1996); *Overcoming The Religious Spirit* (Charlotte, NC: Morning Star Publications, 1996).

Sandford, John and Paula, *The Elijah Task* (Tulsa, OK: Victory House, 1977).

Yocum, Bruce, *Prophecy, Exercising the Prophetic Gifts of the Spirit in the Church Today* (Ann Arbor: Servant Publications, 1976).

Perhaps the best periodical on prophetic issues is published by Morning Star, *The Morning Star Journal*, PO Box 369, Pineville, NC 28134.

Of general relevance:

Dawson, Jon, *Healing America's Wounds* (Ventura CA: Regal Books, 1994).

Fox, George, *An Autobiography*, Edited with an Introduction and notes by Rufus M. Jones.

Guyon, Jeanne, *Experiencing the Depths of Jesus Christ* (Gardiner Maine: Christian Books, 1975).

Habig, Marion A. (ed), *St Francis of Assisi Writings and Early Biographies* (Chicago: Franciscan Herald Press, 1983).

Lewis, C.S., *The Narnia Chronicles* (available in many different editions).

Richardson, Don, *Eternity in Their Hearts* (Venture, CA: Regal Books, 1981, revised 1984).

Upham, T.C., *Life, Religious Opinions and Experiences of Madame Guyon* (London: Allenson and Co, Ltd., 1905).

Von Matt, Leonard and Hauser, Walter, *St Francis of Assisi*, tr. Sebastian Bullough, O.P. (Chicago: Henry Regnery Company, 1956).

Wall, Steve and Arden, Harvey, *Wisdomkeepers: Meeting with Native American Spiritual Elders* (Hillsboro, Oregon: Beyond Words Publishing, 1990).

Andy and Jane Fitz-Gibbon
can be contacted at:

In Christ Ministries Trust
PO Box 27
Hexham
Northumberland
NE46 3RD

In Christ Ministries Inc
PO Box 4973
Ithaca
NY 14852
USA

e-mail: icm@icmi.org
Web: www.icmi.org